Business Object Design and Implementation
OOPSLA '95 Workshop Proceedings

Springer

London
Berlin
Heidelberg
New York
Barcelona
Budapest
Hong Kong
Milan
Paris
Santa Clara
Singapore
Tokyo

J. Sutherland, D. Patel, C. Casanave, G. Hollowell
and J. Miller (Eds)

Business Object Design and Implementation

OOPSLA '95 Workshop Proceedings
16 October 1995, Austin, Texas

 Springer

Dr Jeff Sutherland
269 Highland Avenue
Winchester
MA 01890-3105, USA

Cory Casanave
Data Access Corporation
14000SW 119 Avenue
Miami
FL33186-6017, USA

Joaquin Miller
SHL Systemhouse
440 Davis Street, Apt 410
San Francisco, CA94111-2410, USA

Dr Philip Patel
Centre for Information and Office Systems
School of Computing, Information
    Systems and Mathematics
South Bank University
103 Borough Road
London SE1 0AA, UK

Glenn Hollowell
Texas Instruments
8390/1BJ Freeway
PO Box 655303 MS 3663
Dallas, TX 75243, USA

ISBN-13:978-3-540-76096-2   e-ISBN-13:978-1-4471-0947-1
DOI: 10.1007/978-1-4471-0947-1

Springer-Verlag Berlin Heidelberg New York
British Library Cataloguing in Publication Data
Business object design and implementation : Oopsla '95 Workshop proceedings
    1. Business - Computer programs 2. Object-oriented databases 3. Object-oriented
    programming (Computer science)
    I. Sutherland, Jeffrey V.
    658'.05'511
ISBN-13:978-3-540-76096-2   e-ISBN-13:978-1-4471-0947-1

Library of Congress Cataloging-in-Publication Data
A Catalog record for this book is available from the Library of Congress

Typesetting: Camera ready by authors

34/3830-543210 Printed on acid-free paper

Contents

Introduction
Dilip Patel and Jeff Sutherland 1

Business Objects Standards and Architectures

Business-Object Architectures and Standards
Cory Casanave 7

The Object Technology Architecture: Business Objects for
Corporate Information Systems
Jeff Sutherland 29

The OMG Business Object Facility and the OMG Business Object
Oliver Sims 37

An Architecture Framework: From Business Strategies to
Implementation
William F Hertha, Jim E Bennett, Frank J Post and Ian M Page 47

Object Oriented Technology and Interoperability

An Architectural Framework for Semantic Inter-Operability in
Distributed Object Systems
Rainer Kossmann 63

Semantics: The Key to Interoperability
Stéphane Poirier and Colin Ashford 69

Business Objects Applications

Object Business Modelling, Requirements and Approach
Guus Ramackers and Dai Clegg 77

Implementing Business Objects: CORBA Interfaces for Legacy
Systems
Thomas Grotehen and René Schwarb 87

Modeling Business Enterprises as Value-Added Process
Hierarchies with Resource-Event-Agent Object Templates
Guido L Geerts and William E McCarthy 94

Managing Object Oriented Software Development Projects

SCRUM Development Process
Ken Schwaber 117

Experiences with a Manufacturing Framework
S L Stewart and J A St Pierre 135

Business Application Components
Tom Digre 151

Author Index 167

Contributors List

Dilip Patel
Centre for Information and Office Systems, School of Computing,
Information Systems and Mathematics, South Bank Universlty,
103 Borough Road, London SE1 0AA, UK

Cory Casanave
Data Access Corporation, 1400SW 119 Avenue, Miami, FL 33186, USA

Jeff Sutherland
269 Highland Avenue, Winchester, MA 01890, USA
Formerly at:
Individual, Inc., 8 New England Executive Park West, Burlington,
MA 01803, USA

Oliver Sims
email: olivers@cix.compulink.co.uk

William F Hertha
Jim E Bennett
Frank J Post
Ian M Page
Architecture Services, Canadian Imperial Bank of Commerce,
901 King St. W. 7th Floor, Commerce Court, Postal Station 'A', Toronto,
Ontario, Canada

Rainer Kossmann
P O Box 3511, Station C, Ottawa, Ontario, Canada, K1Y 4H7

Stéphane Poirier
Colin Ashford
Bell-Northern Research Ltd, P O Box 3511, Station C, Ottawa, Ontario,
Canada, K1Y 4H7

Guus Ramackers
Dai Clegg
Oracle Corporation, European Development Centre, Oracle Park,
Guildford Road, Bittams Lane, Chertsey KT16 9RG, UK

Thomas Grotehen
University of Zurich, grotehen@ifi.unizh.ch

René Schwarb
SYSTOR AG, Schwarb.Rene@ch.swissbank.com

Guido L Geerts
William E McCarthy
Department of Accounting, N270 North Business Complex,
Michigan State University, East Lansing, MI 48824, USA

Ken Schwaber
Advanced Development Methods, 131 Middlesex Turnpike, Burlington,
MA 01803, USA

S L Stewart
James A St Pierre
US Department of Commerce, Technology Administration,
National Institute of Standards and Technology, Gaithersburg, MD 20899,
USA

Tom Digre
Business Application Components, Information Technology Group,
Texas Instruments, Inc., 6620 Chase Oaks Blvd., MS 8417, Plano,
TX 75023, USA

Introduction

Dilip Patel and Jeff Sutherland

Email: dilip@vax.sbu.ac.uk, jsutherland@bix.com

The software industry over the past ten years has been actively using object technology in building effective desktops for end user computing. This use has also been taken up by software package builders (word processors, spreadsheets and general applications). The benefits acquired are seen in terms of increased productivity and the ability to reuse components to enhance products, in order to meet new demands from the users. The problem is that object technology has made little impact on the core applications which support businesses in carrying out their tasks. The reasons for this may be as a result of:

- The business community having little confidence in innovative concepts and new technology.

- The business community taking a short term view that their investment in existing systems adequately meets their day to day business operations.

- Major suppliers of business solutions have not appreciated the power of object technology in terms of productivity and maintainability.

More recently the object oriented research community and software and hardware vendors have realised that, if object technology is going to make any impact on commercial applications, it needs to develop techniques of encapsulating chunks of code which equate to something real in business terms. If this can be achieved, there is a potential for it being used far more freely and flexibly. It can be used independently, distributed around client/server networks, or it can be combined with other objects and assembled into applications. The tasks of specifying what constitutes a business object, enterprise model, interoperability and interface services still need to be resolved. The Object Management Group (OMG) has been addressing these issues by specifying the Interface Definition Language (IDL) standard, which would allow business objects from all suppliers to interoperate both within and between applications, irrespective of the language they are written in. If this is achieved, then the business objects will be recognised by the software that meets the OMG's common object request broker architecture (Corba) standards. Casanave in his paper proposes a connecting middle layer between the CORBA facilities and the need for a standard to support vertical applications. The philosophy of the paper highlights the need to identify the advantages and practicalities of standards, and their requirement.

Sutherland takes a practical view of business objects and his paper complements the paper by Casanave. Sutherland sets a rationale for business objects in terms of reduced life cycle time and return on investment. The paper uses a simple order entry business object to illustrate the necessary components for a client server architecture to be realised.

The paper by Sims looks at Common Business Objects from an implementation point of view and concentrates on clarifying the role of Business Object Facility in terms of interoperability and simplicity. Sims concludes by highlighting the need to define standards in six general areas to address the issues of interoperability and simplicity, for end user application development.

Hertha *et. al.,* propose a framework for information handling and implementation within the context of business needs. The framework is based on three related models (the Reference Model, the EndState Model and the Deployable model), each comprising of four tiers (Strategy Tier, Process Tier, Application Object Tier and Technology Tier). The paper describes the interrelationships between the three models, and the interconnectivity of the four tiers.

Kossman proposes a framework for Semantic Interoperability in real-time object oriented systems. The approach is based on the use of semantic extensions, the notion of covers and a three level architectural schema comprising of views, conceptual and implementation levels.

Poirier and Ashford addresses the issues of interoperability and portability from a modelling perspective. They argue in their paper for a common information model based on a common understanding of the semantics of data and the semantics of changes of data. They illustrate their approach by drawing an analogy between building architectures and telecommunication architectures.

If business objects are going to make a strategic impact on large industrial based projects, the paradigm need to be supported by CASE tools. Ramackers' and Clegg's paper addresses this issues by discussing the prototype Case Tool based on the integration of business process re-engineering, workflow requirements, enterprise modelling and object oriented analysis. The main focus of their approach is to provide set of tools to make modelling of the business environment easier for domain experts and end users.

Existing or legacy systems contain the majority of the business functionality required for the business to run. The approach described by Grotehen and Schwarb provides a mechanism of rejuvenating these systems. It describes their experiences of implementing business objects using the CORBA architecture to interface with legacy systems.

Geerts and McCarthy's paper reports on the applications of object oriented concepts in modelling the value-added processes of a business enterprise.

The paper concentrates on describing the resource-event-agent model using a simple example and shows the benefits to be gained from an object oriented implementation.

In the object oriented community there is a lively debate in the area of project management. The paper by Schwaber uses the rugby metaphor to describe how the software development process can be planned and executed. The paper outlines in detail the major stages and steps in the SCRUM methodology and its advantages over traditional management techniques.

Stewart and St. Pierre take a hands on approach to their paper. The paper discusses the use of the Computer Integrated Manufacturing framework on the shop floor, to help reduce costs, and increase reuse through object technology. They present a roadmap for adoption and use of the CIM framework. The paper highlights the need for common standards and outlines the stages, tasks, and tools for specifying, reaching consensus, and testing and certification.

Digre proposes a component based architecture, as a means of decreasing software development life cycle. He compares this approach to the semiconductor industry and suggests the problem can be described as a need to reduce the 'surface area' of complexity exposed at any level in the architecture. He proposes a layered approach to software development, which incorporates monolothic, client/server and distributed applications to support vertical problem domains on which enterprise integration models can be built for end user manipulation.

This set of 12 papers represents some of the leading research and experience in building business object frameworks in North America, Europe, and the Soviet Union. The wide variety of papers presented and the high level of expertise at the workshop led to a consensus on several important issues:

- In the future, cycle time will be the most critical issue for business operations. The speed with which new or enhanced products and services can be developed and delivered to the marketplace will determine market share and profitability.

- Products and services will be increasingly supported by software components. Most of these components must be reused from previous development efforts in order to meet required cycle times. This requires major advances in component interoperability and availability. A model for this activity exists in the custom chip industry which is already selling software components packaged as hardware (Digre).

- A radical reversal in the current approach to software engineering is required to meet market demands. Currently, systems have tight coupling between software components (inflexible systems), and loose coupling between analysis, design, and implementation (leading to excessive cost and delivery times, as well as poor fit of software to user requirements). In the future, Business Process Reengineering methods will be tightly coupled with object-oriented analysis and design. Most of the code which is currently written by hand will be generated from design, or reusable components will eliminate the need to write it.

- Advances in the software development process are required to dramatically improve productivity in a component based development environment. In particular, previous methods have assumed software development as a controlled process rather than an empirical process. Component based object systems are not Turing machines because of their event driven nature and as a result are not fully specifiable.

- The process control industry has developed methods to deal with these types of empirical processes and these methods must be applied to software development using a SCRUM approach (Schwaber).

- Component based architectures will be built from replaceable units of functionality that reduce the surface area of systems that are doubling in complexity each year. Large grain components will have clear sets of responsibilities or roles, and expose semantics of the business as well as syntax of interfaces (Digre).

- There are specific design patterns that should be implemented throughout business systems that will substantially improve reusability and rigor in business systems logic. The "Give/Take" pattern that has been standardized by accounting research should be rigorously implemented in all business systems and mandated in all accounting systems (Geerts, *et. al.*) As much as 50% of the typical business application could be built from recursively implementing this pattern. Many companies (even banks) have trouble balancing their books or accurately determining the current status of business operations because of failure to implement this pattern properly in their business software systems.

Design patterns, business object frameworks, and loosely coupled plug compatible components, combined with radical reengineering of the software development process enable dramatic gains in software productivity before the year 2000. The OOPSLA Business Object Design and Implementation Workshop will continue to meet annually to support and participate in this revolutionary change occuring in the software industry. These developments are accelerated by the rapid evolution of the Internet and the World Wide Web and this will be a key topic in the 1996 workshop.

Business Objects Standards and Architectures

Business-Object Architectures and Standards

Cory Casanave

Data Access Corporation
14000 S.W. 119 Avenue, Miami, Florida 33186 USA
cory_casanave@omg.org

ABSTRACT: *Business information systems have become an integrated part of the modern enterprise and as such are required to enable the enterprise to serve and adapt to complex and dynamic business needs. An application architecture based on "business objects" is proposed as a way to build information systems to better meet these needs. Business objects are defined as components of the information system that directly represent the business model.*

KEY WORDS: *business object, interoperability, OMG BOMSIG, CORBA, Business model.*

BIOGRAPHY: Cory Casanave is the founder and a co-president of Data Access Corporation, a developer of object-oriented application-development tools, and chairman of the OMG Business Object Domain Task Force (BODTF) as well as a member of the OMG board of directors.

1. Introduction

The quality of a company's information system has become recognized as a strategic corporate advantage. Information systems have become the backbone of the modern enterprise and as such are crucial to its functioning. An organization with the appropriate information tools can take advantage of business opportunities quickly and can adapt itself to changing business requirements.

Despite advances in hardware, software, client/server technology, right-sizing, distributed computing, and better methodologies, corporate information processing continues to fight the complexity, inflexibility, and poor performance of its current mix of solutions.

As the enterprise has become more dependent on its information-processing capability, this same growth of dependence has put stress on that very capability. Poor performance, software backlogs and inflexible systems are, unfortunately, the norm.

Many solutions have come (and some have gone) to help with this problem. Some of these solutions—the ones that hold the most hope—are difficult to integrate and move to from existing technologies. Client/server and distributed-object computing in particular are seen as hopeful solutions—and are hard to integrate.

Products, services, and techniques that help overcome these problems can be critical to the success of the enterprise. OMG Business Objects and the Business-Application

Architecture are intended to enable such products, services and techniques by creating a standard framework for business applications, using OMG's CORBA.

It is not the intent of this paper to define or specify a business-application architecture or a business-object protocol. Rather, it is the intent to identify the advantages of, need for, and practicality of such standards in order to foster further work in this area.

1.1 Terms used

Terms used in the Business-Object domain correspond to terms used for similar (but lower-level) concepts in other disciplines. The following table relates terms used in this model to the other domains.

Business Objects	Object-Oriented Engineering	Software	SmallTalk
Business Object	Entity		Model
Presentation	Interface		Presentation
Business-Process Object	Controller		Control

2. OMG Business Objects

Object-oriented systems have existed for about twenty years, but have only gained widespread acceptance in the last five years. In particular, objects have come to dominate user interfaces and system programming. Objects are visible to users as icons, boxes, and windows on the screen that they manipulate directly. This style of user interface (originally developed by Xerox PARC) has spawned a huge advance in the ease of use, esthetics, and power of end-user software.

Objects have also been used extensively by advanced programmers in systems software and applications. Objects are now part of the implementation of almost every major piece of software. While not fully exploited, object-oriented programming is currently helping make software more reliable and reusable.

Paradoxically, objects have not been widely used to represent the business itself. A business can be "modeled" in terms of objects that make up and reflect it. Objects can represent inventory and invoices, customers, and salespeople. Objects can also represent events in a business, such as purchases, sales, and other types of transactions.

Modeling the world as objects and then implementing them in an object-oriented system is the basis of object-oriented technology. It is time that the power and ease of understanding inherent in objects be applied to the business itself. Anything that is related to the finances, products, or customers of an enterprise can be a business object and work as part of a cooperative business-object system.

Put another way, business objects represent things, processes or events that are meaningful to the conduct of the business. Business objects can be distinguished from programming objects such as arrays and I/O channels or from user-interface objects such as buttons and windows. Business objects can also be distinguished from system objects such as your word-processing program. Business objects make sense to business people.

2.1 Definition of a Business Object

A <u>business object</u> is a representation of a thing active in the business domain, including at least its business name and definition, attributes, behavior, relationships, rules, policies and constraints. A business object may represent, for example, a person, place, event, business process, or concept. Typical examples of business objects are: employee, product, invoice and payment.
The business-object abstraction, which models the real world, is represented by an object in the information system. Each such object in the information system is a component of that information system and must be supported by a technology infrastructure. [Burt 95]

2.2 Description of an OMG Business Object

> The following *Description of an OMG Business Object* has been adopted by OMG BOMSIG, and is included here for reference [Burt 95].

OMG Business Objects are representations of the nature and behavior of real-world things or concepts in terms that are meaningful to the business. Customers, products, orders, employees, trades, financial instruments, shipping containers, and vehicles are all examples of real-world concepts or things that could be represented by Business Objects.

Business Objects add value over other representations by providing a way of managing complexity, giving a higher-level perspective, and packaging the essential characteristics of business concepts more completely. We can think of Business Objects as actors, role-players, or surrogates for the real world things or concepts that they represent.

Business Objects can act as participants in business processes, because as actors they can perform the required tasks or steps that make up business processes. These Business Objects can then be used to design and implement systems in such a way that these systems exhibit and continue to maintain a close resemblance to the business that they support. This alignment is maintained because object technology allows the development of objects in software that mirror their counterparts in the real world.

Business Objects allow an enterprise to communicate, model, design, implement, distribute, evolve and market the software technology that will enable them to run their business. The implications of Business Objects include:

- **Communication:** Business Objects provide common terms and ideas at a level of detail which can be shared among business and technical people to articulate and understand the business in business terms.
- **Modeling:** Business Objects have certain characteristics and behavior which enables them to be used naturally in modeling business processes, and the relationships and interactions between business concepts.
- **Design:** Business Objects represent real-world things and concepts which enable design effort to be concentrated in manageable chunks.
- **Implementation:** Business Objects have late and flexible binding and well-defined interfaces so that they can be implemented independently.
- **Distribution:** Business Objects are independent so that they can be distributed as self-contained units to platforms with suitable installed infrastructure.
- **Evolution:** Business Objects can be used in a variety of roles and evolve with the needs of the business. They provide a means for integrating, migrating and evolving existing applications.

- **Marketability:** Business Objects have the potential to be commercially distributed and combined with Business Objects from other sources to facilitate a market in Business Objects.

More formally, a Business Object and its component parts are defined as:

- **Business object** : a representation of a thing active in the business domain, including at least its business name and definition, attributes, behavior, relationships and constraints. A business object may represent, for example, a person, place, or concept. The representation may be in a natural language, a modeling language, or a programming language.
- **Business name:** the term used by business experts to classify a business object.
- **Business definition:** a statement of the meaning and purpose assigned to a business object by business experts.
- **Attributes:** facts about the business object relevant to fulfilling its business purpose.
- **Behavior:** the actions a business object is capable of performing to fulfill its purpose, including: recognizing events in its environment, changing its attributes, and interacting with other business objects.
- **Relationship** : an association between business objects that reflects the interaction of their business purposes.
- **Business Rules** : constraints which govern the behavior, relationships, and attributes of a business object.

2.3 Business Objects Are Not DBMS Tables

Business Objects may, at first, seem much like tables in a relational DBMS, since tables also represent business information. In some simpler cases, there may be a direct correspondence between a business object and a DBMS table. But in most cases, the business objects will be implementing rules and processes beyond the capability of a DBMS. They may be combining multiple tables, managing distribution or managing information that is not even stored in a DBMS (like online stock price quotations). Business objects represent multiple tables, processes and rules at a higher level than the DBMS table.

2.4 Business Objects and Legacy Systems

Business objects can be built using any form of new development tool or they can be built on top of existing software.

For example, let's assume you have an application with 800 users running on a proprietary DBMS and there is just no way for you to flip a switch and have these users run on a newly designed system. However, you would like to add some new functions today and then transition to a new, more-powerful DBMS over time—**how?**

A business-object "wrapper" is written in the language of the existing DBMS (business objects do **not** have to be implemented in an object-oriented language) using a business-object framework. The relationships, rules, and procedures for using the object are implemented as part of the business object using the existing libraries and methods of the legacy application. This new business object can then be used as part of the new business-object architecture while still using the existing legacy application. Critical new functions can be added on top of the business objects. This is using object techniques without changing the legacy programming environment. Conceptually, the user interface of the old program can be replaced by the Business-Object framework.

New presentations are designed with a business-object toolkit or another language to give users a consistent view of their applications through the business objects. These new presentations can be used at the same time as the original programs.

As time permits, the legacy application can be replaced—piece by piece, until it is gone. Once the legacy application is gone, you are free to re-implement the business object with more-current DBMS systems and tools *without changing the other business objects or applications (presentations) that depend on it.*

Legacy applications may be wrapped at the DBMS level (as in the above example) or at the application level. Business-object wrappers may communicate directly with the legacy programs, which may or may not store information in a DBMS.

It is a unique feature of the business-object architecture that it works so well for building new applications **and** providing a transition strategy for legacy applications and data.

Frameworks, adaptors, and re-engineering tools can be produced to assist with the transformation of legacy systems in any language, on any DBMS or transaction processor.

3. The Business-Application Architecture

The Business-Application Architecture (BAA) represents an application architecture and a protocol for "cooperative business objects" [Sims 95]. It is not the architecture of the business or of a specific application, but an architecture for how to represent and implement business concepts as business objects. The BAA is the "glue" that binds the business model with the technology. The BAA, together with an appropriate implementation, will provide a architecture in which business-object attributes, relationships, business rules, and application rules can be implemented. Objects implemented in this way will then be interoperable with other business objects that were implemented in this way.

All information systems have an architecture. That architecture may be formalized and structured, or it may be informal and implied. But for a system to operate, there must be agreed-to conventions, structures, and protocols - this is the architecture. Most "application-development systems" combine an application architecture with tools and sometimes a language to help implement that architecture. The architecture becomes part of the way you use the system or language.

The application architecture can be thought of as that layer between the high-level business objects being implemented and the low-level languages, operating systems, object-request brokers, and DBMS systems. As part of the architecture, a "protocol" exists for the components of that architecture to interact The protocol includes an object model, all interfaces, rules, constraints and ordering considerations.

The BAA is **not** a standard business model; it does not attempt to specify the standard or common components, object structures, or processes in a business. It is a standard way to represent any business model as a structure of executable distributed objects.

3.1 How Does the BAA Fit with Tools and Languages?

The business-application architecture does not attempt to specify the correct or best method for implementing business objects. Any combination of computer languages, 4GLs, design tools, frameworks, rule-based systems, and expert systems may be employed to implement a business object. Frameworks and other forms of tools and components are anticipated as products that assist developers or users in defining and implementing business objects that enable the business-object protocol. The BAA and underlying technologies provide a structural layer that allows differing implementation vehicles to work together in the same businesses.

It is expected that higher-level interfaces will be provided so as to hide the highly technical Interface-Description Language (IDL) interfaces from application developers. These higher-level tools and frameworks will provide standard BAA-to-IDL interfaces as a "framework" that application developers can use more easily. The high-level frameworks and tools will provide interfaces appropriate for directly defining business objects, attributes, relations, and business rules. In that these high-level interfaces may interoperate via the BAA protocol, we do not expect these interfaces to require standards of their own.

Note: It is possible for developers to create business objects that directly implement the BAA protocol; however, this protocol must expose some of the complexities inherent in a distributed-object system and for this purpose, implementation frameworks and intermediate components are useful in simplifying the job of the application developer. However, developers are free to use (or extend) the BAA protocol directly for special needs.

For support of legacy systems, business-object frameworks may be built for COBOL, RPG-II, IMS, and CICS. While the "source code" for these systems would appear completely different, the resultant application architecture would be the same and the objects would be interoperable.

3.2 How Does the BAA Fit with Other Application Architectures?

Many application architectures exist for both business and non-business applications. In that such architectures must be able to co-exist with each other and the BAA, the BAA must be sufficiently general to facilitate the interaction of BAA applications with applications of other architectures. The "wrapping" technique previously discussed in connection with legacy applications provides the capability to implement the BAA protocol in conjunction with other architectures—it is **not** an exclusive option. Thus the BAA is intended to provide the interaction protocol for application components in a variety of architectures.

Application architectures outside the business domain generally become part of the implementation of business concepts represented as business objects. For example, while a software-development company may monitor a project with a configuration-management system that uses its own application architecture (such as PTCE), the company's business system may refer to a single entity, which is the development project for that application. The implementation of the "project" business object may use the configuration-management system to provide business information (such as project status) to the business system.

It is unclear at this time whether the BAA can be sufficiently general to represent **all** business applications. It is our hope that other architectures can be built as **extensions** to the BAA rather than **alternatives** to the BAA. Such a determination can only be made after further work is done in this area.

4. Advantages of OMG Business Objects and the BAA

4.1 Flexibility

Maintaining a simple, standard interface to objects relevant to your business makes the information facility much more flexible. Changes in business policies or structure can be reflected directly by the business objects, and applications based on these will frequently adapt automatically to the changes. New business objects and business structures can be developed and deployed while still maintaining the old interfaces for a cross-over period.

Since the implementations of business objects directly reflect the structure of your business, business objects and applications are easier to produce and maintain, providing a more-responsive information-processing facility.

4.2 A single place to put business rules

The rules, policies and procedures of an enterprise can become quite complex and interrelated. By having a single, known place to put each rule (and express it only once!) the management and evolution of your rules, procedures and policies become much less complex.

4.3 High-level

The business objects operate at a "high" level, one that is understood by business people. Entire organizations—and in particular top management, can participate in the design of its information model and business rules without having to be burdened by implementation details. Business Objects use business names and terms.

4.4 Works with legacy systems

Legacy systems and data can be "wrapped" as business objects to become part of the new generation of applications without discarding the value of the legacy applications.

4.5 Insulation from insufficient or transient standards

Standards which were intended to prevent the business from becoming dependent on a particular vendor tend to be frustrated in real-world situations. Information-systems departments seem inevitably to depend on proprietary extensions and features sooner or later that again cause "lock in". With business objects, the enterprise's own information model becomes the standard, insulated from the DBMS or "tool *du jour*". Advances in technology and new standards can be more easily integrated with working systems.

4.6 Open architecture

The business-object architecture is open and extensible. Interfaces and capabilities can be added as required for the business's need. Even the business architecture itself can be implemented on top of any distributed-object standard. As standards come into place, business objects become interoperable and tools can be provided to create and maintain them.

Any type of tool can be used to implement business objects or exploit their existence. Advanced Business Process Re-engineering tools, Workflow systems, CASE tools, 4GLs or 3GLs can all be employed to create or use business objects. The high-level nature of business objects makes them ideal for advanced decision-support systems and report writers.

4.7 Scaleable

Since business objects can employ advanced distribution mechanisms "behind the scenes" and the same or a related business object can be distributed across multiple systems, the architecture is infinitely scaleable. The applications are insulated from changes made to scale the system.

4.8 Reusable components

Business objects represent well-defined reusable components for application development. Reusable components leverage design and development efforts, increasing responsiveness and reducing costs. Business objects may be purchased from third-party vendors and integrated into an existing system.

Since business objects directly represent the business model, reuse becomes natural. The business model and objects (which have a natural order) become the library of reusable components.

4.9 Opens system to "power users"

Since business objects are visible to the "desktop," any program or user can access *and safely manipulate* the objects of the business. Power users and end users get unprecedented accessibility to enterprise resources.

Business objects are safe to manipulate because data integrity and business rules are enforced by the business objects.

4.10 Ideal for business-process re-engineering

Business-process re-engineering (BPR) is heavily dependent on a strong and flexible information system. Business objects are an ideal way to implement an information system that supports BPR. The type of analysis done to "re-engineer" a company can produce the of business model that business objects can implement.

Ivar Jacobson, in his excellent book *Object Advantage* [Jacobson 94], shows how BPR and object-oriented analysis can be combined and are complementary.

4.11 Ease of use

Providing a pre-built application framework places the user in a better position to concentrate on the application problems. Users who are forced to build an application framework "from the ground up" can face a huge effort in design and implementation that has nothing to do with their business problems. A well-thought-out, proven and standard framework can save massive amounts of work. Combine this with the possibility of purchasing pre-built objects and pre-built tools and the user's work is really leveraged!

Business objects use business terms in ways that business people understand. Keeping the terminology in line with the business makes the entire system more understandable.

4.12 Business objects are "happening"

Business objects are a hot topic. The press is talking about them, standards bodies, like the Object Management Group (OMG), are talking about them. IS professionals are asking for the functionality. Vendors are implementing them. Users who currently are trying to use "two-level" client/server systems *know* they need them.

4.13 Standards and the OMG

While products based around this architecture are attractive, standards will make it an industry. By standardizing on the Business-Object Architecture, objects created in diverse systems can interoperate and companies can provide specialized tools to create and maintain the business objects.

The lower "technology" layer is already available and standard as CORBA 2.0. The next layer of standardization can provide the higher-level business-object protocol.

We expect the infrastructure and interface to become standardized by the OMG sometime in 1996. Once this happens, the now-uncoordinated efforts being put into business objects can become cooperative technologies supporting a common application architecture.

Post-OOPSLA update: An RFP for business objects was issued by the OMG on January 11th, 1996 [Casanave 96].

5. How Business Objects Fit into a Business

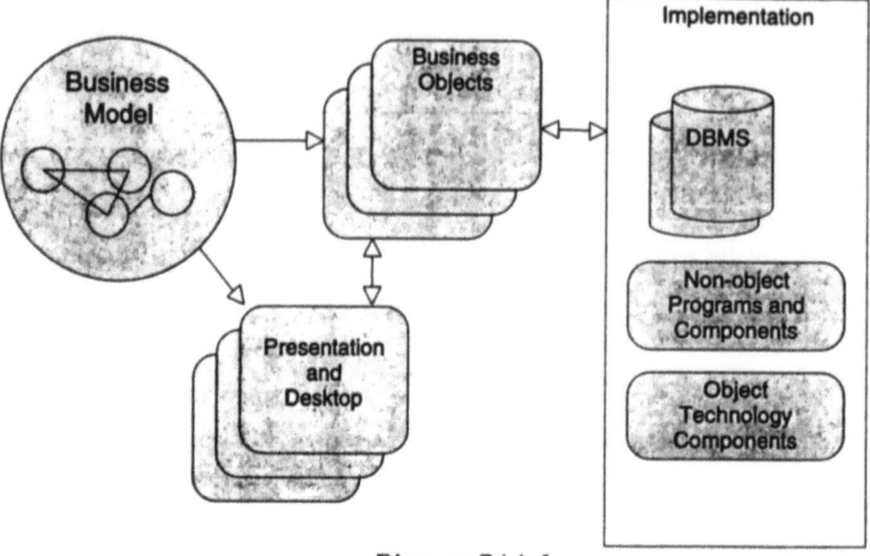

Diagram BAA-1

5.1 The business model

The basis for any business-object system is the "model" of the actual business. This model is built using abstract business objects and processes and/or more-specialized versions of these abstract objects.

This model should include every person, place, thing, event, or transaction that needs to be captured in the information system.

The business processes are likewise identified and modeled as business-process objects.

Once complete, this business model becomes a valuable reference to how your business is organized and operates.

5.2 Business objects and implementation components

Each object in the business model is used to create an executable representation of that object in your computer system. This executable object will contain and encapsulate the information and rules associated with that object and its relationships to other objects.

Some business objects may be implemented on top of existing applications as "wrappers", exposing the legacy application as business objects. Other objects may be implemented using Workflow tools, computer languages or 4GLs. Provided all of the tools and wrappers can "speak" the BAA protocol, consistency of implementation environment is not required.

When used with a traditional DBMS, the executable objects sit between the DBMS and the user interface providing an object-oriented, multi-tier client/server system.

The direct representation of the business model as executable and user-accessible objects is the essence of the business-object concept!

5.3 Presentation and system interfaces

Given the executable business objects, user interfaces are generated to allow users and other applications to view and manipulate the business objects. The business-object user interface becomes the new "look and feel" for your applications. Desktop applications may also interface with the business objects through interfaces such as OpenDoc and OLE.

5.4 The outdated concept of "application"

With a system composed of a set of cooperative business objects, the outmoded concept of monolithic applications becomes irrelevant. Instead, your information system is composed of semi-autonomous but cooperative business objects which can be more easily adapted and changed. This type of *component assembly and reuse* has been recognized as a better way to build information systems.

An application, in terms of business objects, becomes a set of cooperative business objects combined to facilitate business processes.

6. The Requirement for OMG Standards

6.1 Options for an application architecture and framework

Given that an organization wishes to implement a business application, there must be an application architecture. That architecture may be custom, proprietary, or standard. Each approach has its advantages and disadvantages.

6.1.1 Custom

A custom architecture provides maximum internal flexibility to the enterprise. The applications can be designed and tuned to the organization's needs. Since the organization has developed much of its own infrastructure, it is not dependent on as many external suppliers (unless such dependencies are built into the custom framework).

Creating a custom architecture is not a small job. Experience has shown that a highly capable and specialized development team requires one to two years to field a stable infrastructure for applications development in a distributed environment.

The application infrastructure, like all software, will also require costly maintenance and future development. Of course, the application created in a custom environment will not interoperate with external software—considerable effort must be expended to integrate other software and data.

6.1.2 Proprietary

A proprietary application framework may be purchased from a vendor, frequently with some standard business applications. This solves the problems of producing a custom framework, but it does not solve the problems inherent in integrating the system with software that uses another framework.

Many organizations are also concerned about being locked in to a proprietary-framework vendor, since the organization may become very dependent on the provider. However, with a good provider relationship, a proprietary framework may be very productive.

6.1.3 Standard

A standard framework solves the problems of creating a custom framework and becoming locked in to a single vendor. The organization may deal with multiple vendors to supply and support the standard framework.

The standard framework will have a much-larger support base and as such will probably be worked-out and debugged to a greater degree.

The most-important factor in a standard framework is commercial support. Given a standard framework, it is practical to purchase pre-built business objects in an open market. Pre-built objects can be used as-is or enhanced using standard object-oriented techniques, vastly leveraging development. On the tool side, the organization can purchase design and implementation tools, data-analysis tools, languages, libraries and utilities to help use and build applications in a standard framework. Standard desktop applications can interface with the architecture components.

A standard framework also leverages training. A development organization will be better able to find employees and consultants who already understand how the business system operates.

A standard framework can also be expected to have a longer lifetime. While standards take longer to produce, they also last longer. Business applications have an average lifetime of 10-15 years, while some proprietary architectures have a lifetime of one-to-two years. Standards have a lifetime more in keeping with business needs.

The only downside to a standard framework may be flexibility. The framework may not do just what is required in very special conditions. But, the object-oriented paradigm helps here as well, since the standard framework can be extended, as can all object systems.

In short, a standard framework can foster an *industry of business objects*.

6.2 Goals of standardization

The reasons to standardize components of the BAA are directly reflected in the purpose of the OMG...

(a)   to promote a single ob ject-oriented applications-integration environment based on appropriate industry standards;

(b)   to promote a framework for compatible and independent development of applications;

(c)   to enable coordination among applications across heterogeneous networked systems in a multinational, multilingual environment;

(d)   to adopt a core of commercially available implementations of this framework and to promote international market acceptance and use;

(e)   to actively influence the future direction and development of   these core products and technologies; and

(f)   to foster the development of tools and applications that conform to and extend this framework and to provide a mechanism for certifying compliance with the core technologies.

(Article I of the OMG by-laws [OMG 95])

Such a purpose for OMG and the BAA will have a range of advantages...

6.2.1 Synergy

To synergize the work being done in creating business applications and distributed object components into a cooperative industry effort.

6.2.2 Interoperability

To make independently developed business objects interoperable with a minimum of effort.

6.2.3 Federation of systems

To allow diverse business systems to be integrated.

6.2.4 Ease of use

To make the information understandable in business terms and easily meet business needs.

6.2.5 Open market

To foster an open market in business-object-related components, both in pre-built business objects and in tools for using and building business objects.

6.3 What needs to be standard?

With all the advantages of a standard, there is a dark side also. Restrictive standards can stifle innovation, and poor standards can do more harm than good. To minimize the inherent problems of standardization, standards should be *minimal*. That is, they should provide a sufficient level of standardization to meet the goals but no more. Simple, minimal standards are also easier to adopt to future innovation.

Another question of a standard is its scope. We are targeting business applications because of the extreme importance of business data processing and because of the high degree of commonality among business applications. Business applications represent billions of dollars of expenditure worldwide and directly impact the productivity of society—they deserve special attention. Trying to design a framework for all applications may not sufficiently benefit business applications; it may not even be possible. Applications outside the business domain may still use the BAA where appropriate, but it is not the design intent of the BAA. The term "business application" is intended in its more-general sense. The data processing of governments and organizations fall within the domain of the BAA.

6.4 Existing OMG standards

The existing OMG CORBA standards are required to implement a distributed-object business system. They provide the basic mechanisms for creating and using objects in a distributed network.

The existing and proposed OMG standards provide the necessary interfaces for transactions, User interface, events, object lifecycle and object query are all required for a business system. The proposed application architecture must build on and work with the existing standards. For example, the IDL interface to the user interface should conform or work with the user-interface component adopted by OMG common facilities.

The application architecture should build on this existing foundation.

Are the existing standards sufficient? If the existing standards were given to two development teams with the charter of producing the same application, it is unlikely that the above goals would be achieved. Both teams would have to come up with their own answers to fundamental questions like:

- What is the appropriate structure of an application built with these tools?
- How are changes and dependencies propagated?
- Should the user-interface and business rules be together?
- Should the data and business rules be together?
- How does the user interface interact with the data in the business object?
- Where are the business rules put?
- How does an object locate another cooperative object?
- What are the common events that drive the system?
- What happens when a business rule is broken?
- How are errors handled?
- What happens when rules or data change?
- Will the structure scale-up to a running system?

Answering these questions and building the infrastructure to support them is the process of designing the application architecture and framework. Given that no two teams are going to come up with the same rules, the requirement for interoperability will not be achieved, and considerable effort will have been duplicated.

6.5 Required new standards

Two elements are essential to an application architecture and protocol. The architecture represents the components that are used to "model" the business problem and build the system, while the protocol is the set of rules that govern how these components behave and communicate with each other.

For example, in the reference model (Diagram BAA-2), we have presentations and business objects. If users change data in the presentation, how is that change communicated to the business object? If that change violates a business rule, how is that violation communicated to the presentation? Which object is responsible for side effects of that change and how and when are the side effects made visible to the presentation?

Business application are very "state-" (or data-) oriented. That is, business systems are driven by actions changing data and properly propagating the effects of that change. The protocol must provide very clear rules for dealing with that state and propagated effects.

6.5.1 Basic architectural framework

The basic framework outlined in the reference model (Diagram BAA-2) has three components: business objects, business-process objects, and presentations. These are the building blocks of the applications. The same building blocks are used to model the business and to build the application. Each component of the BAA application becomes a subclass of one of these components.

As part of the architectural framework, each of the following must be addressed:

- What the appropriate structure of an application built with these tools is.
- Whether the user-interface and business rules should be together.
- Whether the data and business rules should be together.
- Where the business rules are put.
- What happens when a business rule is broken.
- What happens when rules or data change.
- How the structure will scale up to a running system.

6.5.2 Inter-object protocol

The protocol is the standard IDL interfaces between presentations, business objects, and business-process objects. Anything done to these objects is done through these standard interfaces. The primary purpose of the interface to business objects will be to make and respond to changes in the objects' states. As part of the protocol, business objects should present their *metadata*. Metadata is information about the business object (as distinguished from the data the object is dealing **with**). By having the object present its own metadata, applications can change their behavior based on changes in the metadata, making the entire system more friendly, flexible and dynamic.

As part of the protocol, each of the following issues must be dealt with:

- How are changes and dependencies propagated?
- How does the user interface interact with the business object?
- How does an object locate another cooperative object?
- What are the common events that drive the system?
- How are errors handled?

6.6 What does not need to be standard

Anything that has to do with the e *xpression or implementation* of business objects or presentations should not be standard. The best and most-proper way to express business objects and business rules is still growing and changing; we do *not* need to lock that down in a standard. As long as the objects can implement the desired protocol, our goals are achieved. The following are some of the elements that do not require standards.

- High-level interfaces
- Computer language
- Operating system
- Source code
- Design tools
- Design methods
- Business-rule representations
- Implementation frameworks
- Presentation style
- Custom interfaces

6.7 Domain (application) object interfaces

Once the application architecture has a sufficient level of definition, the question of commonality of specific objects arises. Can we identify common objects like customers, accounts, products and orders and derive common names, attributes and relationships for those objects? Standards for common business objects are not required for the BAA to work, but they would enhance the ability for the objects to interoperate. Standards for business-domain objects is a separate issue from the BAA and is not covered in this paper.

6.8 The RFP

The OMG BOMSIG drafted an RFP (Request For Proposal) [Casanave 96] for common business objects and a Business Object Facility. This RFP was issued by the OMG January 11th, 1996. The RFP items are described as follows:

6.8.1 Common Business Objects

Objects representing those business semantics that can be shown to be common across most businesses.

6.8.2 Business-Object Facility

The infrastructure (application architecture, services, etc...) required to support business objects operating as cooperative application components in a distributed object environment.

The following diagram shows how these facilities fit in the current OMG architecture.

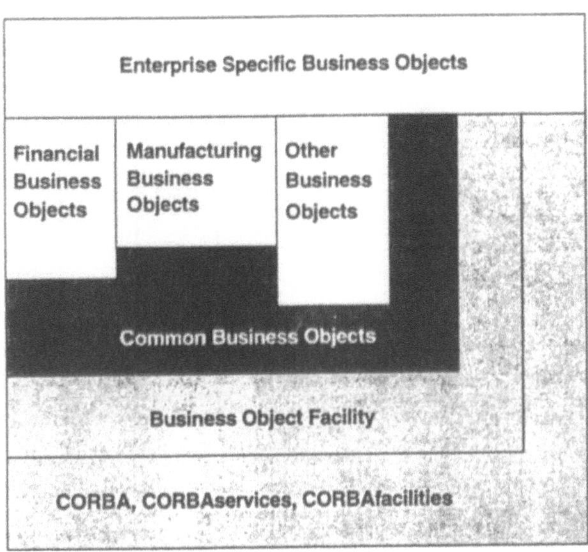

These facilities are seen as the "missing middle layer" between the CORBA facilities as the low-level infrastructure and the needs of standard and custom vertical applications as the high-level.

7. Business Application Architecture Reference Model

The reference model is a general model for business objects intended to encompass multiple interpretations and implementations of this concept. Diagram BAA-2 shows the abstract components of a business-object system and their interrelationships. Specific business-object systems may implement a superset or a subset of this model.

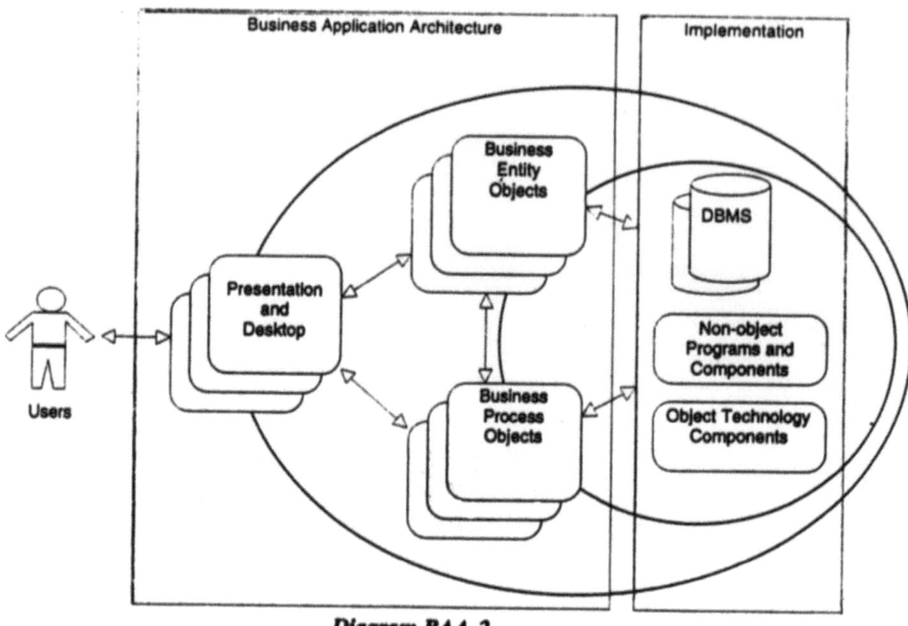

Diagram BAA-2

In this diagram, we can see that the tools used to build "traditional" programs, DBMS systems, technology components, and non-object programs, are encapsulated (shown by the inner circle). Only Business Objects will interface with this layer. Business Objects are encapsulated and made accessible to users by visual presentations and desktop programs. The Business Objects and their presentations comprise the Business Application Architecture.

There are several object-oriented meta-models to draw on for this purpose. A primary candidate is the model contained in the OORAM [Reenskaug 96] methodology. OORAM has the following features:

- the enterprise is modeled in terms of roles and collaborations between roles

- role collaborations and the information model are integrated

- models (frameworks) can be synthesized together

7.1 Components

7.1.1 Applications

Applications in this context are programs that are composed of a set of cooperative business objects. A program may implement one or many presentations and processes that work with business objects.

Any number of applications may be expected to share and reuse a common class of business objects. It is implementation-specific as to whether multiple applications share an instance of a business object.

Note: Not all applications are business-application-architecture applications. Other types of applications may exist for other purposes and architectures.

7.1.2 Business objects

Business objects encapsulate the storage, metadata, concurrency, and business rules associated with a thing, process, or event in a business. Multiple independent but related business objects may cooperate to service one application. Implementations may require different "flavors" of business objects for differing roles, such as: client-local objects and server objects. Business objects are responsible for all aspects of implementation including enforcement of business rules, application rules, data validity, concurrency, and storage. Business Objects are a representation of a thing active in the business domain including, but not limited to, its name and definition, attributes, behavior, relationships, and constraints.

7.1.2.1 Business-entity objects

Entity objects represent the actual things and concepts that make up the business. These are the nouns of the model: the people, places, things, and business events (such as a sale) that model the static state of the enterprise. Entity objects are an object-oriented extension to the concepts found in "ER" modeling and semantic modeling.

7.1.2.2 Business-process objects

Processes represent the flow of work and information throughout the business. These processes act on the business entities to cause the business to function. Business processes may be long-lived (such as an order life cycle) or may be short-lived (such as an end-of-year report). Long-life-cycle business processes are typically part of Business Process Re-Engineering (BPR) analysis.

Business-process objects may be implemented with Workflow systems, business-process managers, object-oriented languages, procedural languages, or interactive process-definition systems. The only requirement on the process implementation/definition environment is that the resulting business process supports the standard BAA interfaces or can be "wrapped" to provide such interfaces.

The executable business-process objects which represent the processes in the information system should not be confused with a Workflow definition that may take a part in implementing a business-process object. A Workflow definition, like any other business rule, is part of defining and implementing the object, not using it.

7.1.3 Presentations

Business objects have a companion —the Business Object Presentation, or "Presentation" for short. Each business object can have multiple presentations for multiple purposes. The presentation is the user's view of the business object for a given purpose. The presentations communicate with the business object in two ways: 1) To transfer information between the presentation and the business object on behalf of the user. 2) To learn how to display and manipulate the information (called "metadata" or, data about the data).

Having the presentations learn about the data from the business object makes them very simple and flexible. If anything about the business object is changed, that change is immediately reflected in the presentations.

Presentations are one type of application that can make use of business objects. Custom applications and automated processes (like Agents) can be part of a business-object system.

Presentations are always run on client machines but, thanks to the distributed-application architecture, the business objects and DBMS systems can run on the client machines, the server, or both. In large systems, the implementation of a single business object can be split into multiple pieces to better optimize performance across large networks. Since the mechanisms of implementing the business object and storing the data are encapsulated "behind the scenes", advanced DBMS distribution, object-oriented DBMSes, concurrency, and replication systems can be added to change the scale of operation without changing the interface to, or use of, the business object. Business objects can "scale" to the capacity of the underlying systems.

7.1.4 Implementation

The implementation components are encapsulated by the business objects. They are not accessed directly by users, processes, or presentations. The business objects use and manipulate DBMS systems, technology components, and non-object programs to implement their functionality.

7.1.4.1 DBMS

The DBMS (or similar repository) is expected to store the representations of business objects and aid in their retrieval and concurrency. Many but not all business objects will use a DBMS to store their states.

7.1.4.2 Non-object programs and components

Business objects can encapsulate non-object or legacy programs so as to provide these older applications with the business-object interface. Existing non-object programs can also be modified to replace their user interface with a business-object interface.

7.1.4.3 Object technology components

Object technology components are the other pieces of technology required to implement the business objects. In the OMG model, these include CORBA, CORBAservices and CORBAfacilities. They also include other applications used to support the business objects.

7.2 Requirements

7.2.1 Encapsulation

The architecture of a business-object system is one in which the data, data storage, business rules and operations relating to each business entity are "encapsulated" (contained in and hidden by) a business object. These business objects have a simple, standard interface that allows them to communicate with other business objects and with business-object presentations (presentations are what users see on terminals and reports). This represents the standard notion of object-oriented encapsulation applied to the business domain.

7.2.2 Responsibilities

Each business object is responsible for managing its own storage (usually in a DBMS), security, maintaining its relationship with other objects, and *implementing and enforcing the policies, procedures and rules of the business as they relate to that business object.* Business objects are information-centric in that they expose and manipulate business information. Business objects are encouraged, but not required, to utilize OMG object services and common facilities for implementation.

7.2.3 Distribution

Business Objects are implemented on top of a standard distributed-object broker such as CORBA (OMG), DSOM (IBM) or COM-OLE2 (Microsoft). These distributed-object systems have only recently become available as industrial-strength products and this technology is key to the business application architecture. The object broker allows **any** program (even your word processor or spreadsheet) to access and manipulate the business objects. Since rules are maintained by the business objects, complete control is exercised over the integrity and validity of the enterprise data. The object broker also allows any object to exist on any computer system and still integrate with the total information-processing infrastructure.

7.2.4 Ease of use

Business objects are intended for use by the developers and users of business applications. As such the design and implementation of business objects must support the requirements of these users. These requirements extend across the entire lifecycle of development from design to maintenance. The interfaces and services provided must make sense to these persons and allow them to define business applications without undue knowledge of, or restriction by, the technology.

7.2.5 Loosely coupled

Business objects exist within the dynamic environment of business. Business changes, merges, separates, and re-engineers. Business objects must cooperate within an environment that supports such dynamic change. As such, these objects must cooperate in ways that preserve the semantics but allow each object to change and grow independently.

7.3 Specialization of business objects

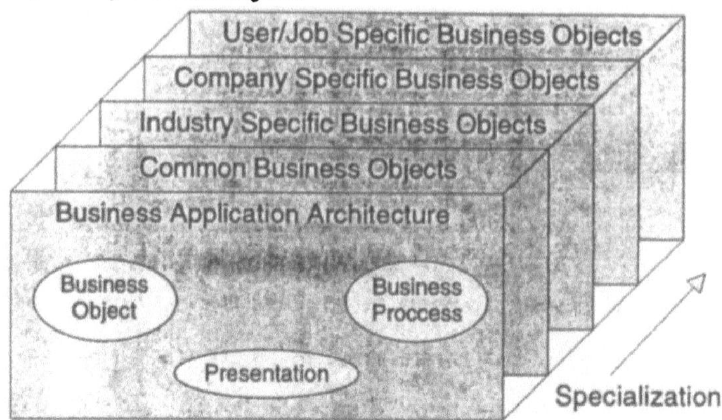

Diagram BAA-3

The generic Business Objects, Business Processes, and Presentations defined in the Business Application Architecture are specialized through common, industry, company, and user business objects.

For example, A Business Object might be specialized to create an "order" object in a general business suite. This order object may then be further specialized in a consulting company to be an "order for consulting services" object. A particular consulting company may add rules and attributes to that consulting-order object to enforce company policy. Finally, a particular department might further specialize the company's consulting-order object for a particular type of service.

The facility for specialization is inherent in the use of objects to represent the business in the information system. The degree of specialization required is driven by the business requirements of the users and the degree to which specialization will enhance business practices.

8. References

[Burt 95] Carol Burt [ed.]: OMG BOMSIG survey with published definition of a business object. OMG document 95-02-04. Www.omg.org

[Casanave 96] Cory Casanave [ed.]: OMG Common Business Objects and Business Object Facility RFP. OMG Document CF/96-01-04. Www.omg.org

[Jacobson 94] Ivar Jacobson, Maria Erricsson, Agneta Jacobson: *The Object Advantage, Business process reengineering with object technology.* Addison Wesley 1994. ISBN 0-201-42289-1

[OMG 95] Object Management Group: Bylaws (not published).

[Reenskaug 96] Trygve Reenskaug with Per Wold and Odd Arild Lehne: *Working with Objects, the OORAM Software Engineering Method.* Manning 1996. ISBN 1-884777-10-4

[Sims 94] Oliver Sims: Business Objects, *Delivering Cooperative Objects for Client-Server* . McGraw-Hill. ISBN 0-07-707957-4

The Object Technology Architecture:
Business Objects for Corporate Information Systems

Dr. Jeff Sutherland
VP Product Development
Individual, Inc.
8 New England Executive Park West
Burlington, MA 01803
Email: jeff.sutherland@individual.com
http://www.tiac.net/users/jsuth/

Abstract. This paper highlights the need for a business object architecture which will allow software to change as rapidly as the underlying business processes, and the benefits of such an architecture, in terms of reduced software development cycle time and increased investment returns. The paper postulates the advantages for organisations who are already developing and implementing globally distributed object systems and how they have a competitive advantage over latecomers.

Key words: Business Objects, Business Object Architectures

Why Business Objects?

> *"RADICAL SURGERY is needed in IS processes. One of the first ideas that will have to go is the whole notion of traditional systems development life cycles." Michael Hammer*[1]

The global market has become an intensely competitive environment moving at an accelerating rate of change. To gain the strategic advantages of speed and flexibility, corporations must remodel their business processes, then rapidly translate that model into software implementations.

Business Process Reengineering (BPR) sets the stage for continuous evolution of business processes to meet rapidly evolving business requirements. Implementation of software systems that support BPR requires Business Objects that can both simulate corporate procedures and translate smoothly into software objects. Well-designed Business Object implementations can be easily modified as the business changes.

What Are Business Objects?

Technically, business objects encapsulate traditional lower-level objects that implement a business process (i.e., they are a collection of lower-level objects that behave as single, reusable units). User interfaces can be thought of as views of large-grained Business Objects. Databases maintain a record of the "state" of Business Objects as they change over time.

---

[1] Hammer, Michael. *Interview by Joseph Maglitta. Computerworld,* 24 Jan 94.

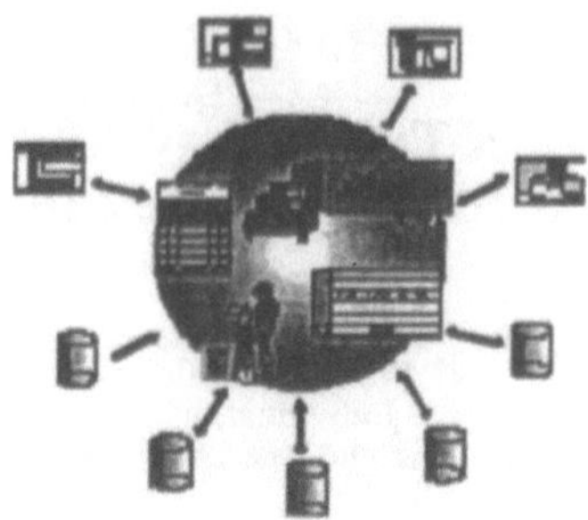

Figure 1: A Business Object

The Need for a Business Object Architecture

As business models are renewed, software architectures must be transformed. A Business Object Architecture (BOA) is an effective solution for dynamic automation of a rapidly evolving business environment.

Dynamic change requires reuse of chunks of business functionality. A BOA must support reusable, plug-compatible business components. The two primary strategies now being used for implementing client/server systems to support reengineering of business processes are Visual 4th Generation Languages and classical object technology. While both of these approaches are better than COBOL, neither of them can implement Business Objects. Visual 4GLs generate the Powerblender Syndrome -- Write all your business logic in proprietary procedural code and embed it in user interfaces or "GUI objects." Classical object technology produces the Rigatoni Effect. Proliferation of objects without constraints on complexity results in a message path explosion within an object system. This produces unmaintainable code. Even experienced object-oriented programmers find it easier to create this problem rather than implement a Business Object Architecture. We don't have spaghetti code in object systems. We have little balls of rigatoni that stick together producing mush, the result of poor design of object components. Classical object technology is really an assembly language that we can use to build a BOA.

Because of these problems, current attempts at software implementation of reenginneered businesses processes are not very successful.

> *"The shining examples of reengineering glory remain few and far between, and a recent study of IT systems-development efforts asserts a failure sinkhole equal to roughly an $80 billion sucking sound." Lew McCreary, Editor, CIO/Webmaster Supplement.*[2]

Reduced Cycle Time Is the Prime Directive

The goal of a Business Object Architecture is rapid deployment of reengineered business processes and rapid redeployment of new or enhanced functionality as the business changes. Dramatic examples of this can be found on Wall Street, where a new financial instrument can be defined, implemented, and traded with a one-week turnaround.

Some of the best data in the industry on productivity has been collected by Capers Jones of Software Productivity Research, Inc.[3] Detailed information has been collected on over 6,000

---

[2] McCreary, Lew. Mutate (editorial). *Webmaster: A Supplement to CIO Magazine*, Sep/Oct 1995, p. 7.

products and is used as a reference database for software project estimation. The Software Productivity Research (SPR) data indicates that reusability of code for C is 15%. This reuse factor is about the same for other 3rd and 4th generation languages. For an object-oriented language like Smalltalk, it is possible to get 50% reuse in year 2 and 80% reuse is achievable in year 3.

SPR data show that COBOL is twice as productive as C. A 4th Generation Language doubles the productivity of COBOL. Smalltalk can be twice as productive as a 4GL, but only when 80% reuse is achievable.

Return on Investment Depends on Reduced Cycle Time

Flexibility and Adaptability

The primary reason many large users adopt object technology is not reduced costs of implementation. The largest returns are captured by faster time to market with new products and services, and faster enhancement and extension of those services compared to competitors. For example, last year a $500M division of Bankers Trust in New York increased revenue by 30-40% and saved the bank hundreds of thousands of dollars in inaccurately entered trades using Object Studio, an advanced development environment for Business Object design and implementation.[4]

Scalability

Business Object Architectures support scalability better than conventional systems. A small system can be scaled up to large numbers of users and gigabytes of data faster, easier, and cheaper.

On a large European project in 1990[5], James Martin Associates was hired to provide an independent review of a Business Object system by the world's largest aircraft leasing company. They reported that as the object system was scaled into production and performance bottlenecks forced redesign of subsystems, the object model could be restructured quickly to improve performance without compromising system design. No other technology they had seen could do this, and they reported that scalability was the greatest benefit of object technology.

Ease of scalability depends on a visual representation of an object model. A Business Object Architecture is largely generated from the design and reengineered at the design level. Business Object Management Tools are required because novices cannot build a BOA without them and experts will not spend the time required to do it manually.

Reusability

Flexibility, reduced cycle time, and lower costs are all dependent on reusability of Business Objects. Reusability has been difficult to achieve on early object-oriented projects because class libraries are not inherently very reusable. Searching through a class library, and understanding the details of code used to build the classes, can often cost more than rebuilding the classes from scratch.

---

[3] Jones, T. Capers. *Table of Programming Languages and Levels, Version 8*. Software Productivity Research, Inc., 2 June, 1995 (http://www.spr.com/)

[4] Scheier, Robert L. Object-Oriented Tool Deployment: Bankers Trust Co.: Object tools put trading on fast track. *PC Week, 7 March 1994.*

[5] Gardner, J., Sutherland, J.V. *Report on Buyer Furnished Equipment Development History and Level of Effort.* Object Databases, Cambridge, Mass., November, 1990

This problem is now being solved by Business Object Management Tools that capture the design, documentation, and code as a system is being developed. Changes at the code level are automatically synchronized with design documents. Components built of groups of collaborating objects are specified at the business level. These components are objects that have all the characteristics of fine-grain objects allowing them to be reused as is, or easily modified through specialization through inheritance.

Building Business Object Components

A group of objects is the ideal unit of reuse. These groups of objects should behave as a higher-level business process and have a clearly specified business language interface. Business components are encapsulated with a protocol that allows efficient communication with other objects on the network.

Consider a typical client/server application like an order entry system. This system takes a Purchase Order as input and produces a validated order as output. The internals of this component should be a black box to the external world. The resulting order is input for another subsystem or, alternatively, an exception condition is raised if the Purchase Order is not valid for processing.

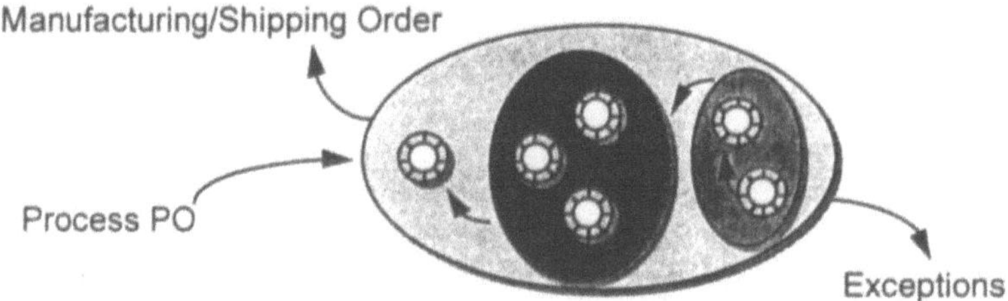

Figure 2: An Order Entry Business Object

To support plug-compatible reuse, a business component must be encapsulated in two directions. The external world must not know anything about component internals, and the internals must not know anything about external components, other than allowing interested objects to register for notification of specific events or exception conditions.

The internals of a business component are made of other encapsulated business components. For example, when a Purchase Order passes through the membrane of the Order Entry business object, an internal component must see it, validate it, look up customer information, inventory availability and catalogue pricing, and build an order that is consistent with business rules and procedures. Each of these tasks is accomplished by embedded components, many of them communicating with external data sources.

External databases must be encapsulated as Business Objects or reuse will not be easily achievable. There must be a database access component that causes values from any kind of database to materialize as objects inside the business component. Whether object-oriented, relational, or other database access is required, a set of class libraries designed to automate this interface will result in a major savings in development resources.[6]

---

[6] Sutherland JV, Pope M, Rugg K. The Hybrid Object-Relational Architecture (HORA): An Integration of Object-Oriented and Relational Technology. *Proceedings of the 1993 ACM/SIGAPP Symposium on Applied Computing*, Indianapolis, 14-16 Feb 1993. Deaton E et al (Eds) ACM Press, pp 326-333.

An Order Entry business object will typically have multiple user interfaces. A clerk may be taking the order over the phone, entering purchase information, validating customer records and credit data, and reviewing an order for consistency and customer acceptance. Other users may require different presentation screens. User interfaces are difficult and time consuming to build at the code level. Today, much of this process can be automated. They should be encapsulated as separate objects that communicate by message passing to the Order Entry object. Failure to do this will limit reuse and waste valuable programmer time on laborious, time consuming maintenance tasks. Users should be able to create interface objects with simple object-oriented tools. Subsequently, the programmer should be able to easily snap user interface objects onto the Order Entry object.

A simple Order Entry client/server component has at least three large-grained components, one or more presentation objects, a business component that models the business process, and a database access component that shields the application developer from database access languages, database internals, and network communications (see Figure 3).

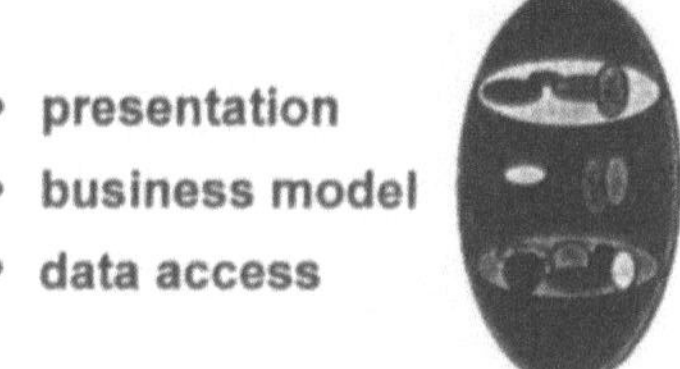

Figure 3: Client-Server Component

Business Object programmers focus their efforts on building business components, or large-grained Business Objects, which can be easily distributed on the network.

Distributing Business Objects

System evolution will invariably distribute these Business Objects to maximize network performance and processor utilization, and to ensure proper control, integrity, and security of information. Business reengineering implies implementing a distributed environment where components encapsulating business functionality can be migrated to nodes on the network that allow maximum flexibility, scalability, and maintainability of a Business Object system.

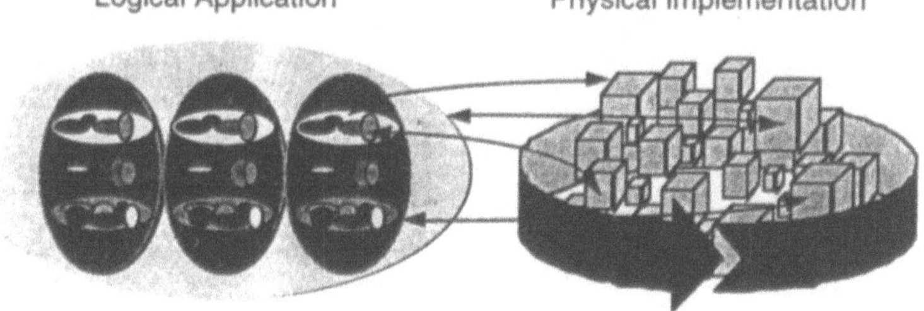

Figure 4: Application Business Object with Nested Client/Server Components

Business objects made up of nested components allow distribution of these components across a network. Figure 4 shows the logical application as a coherent set of nested client/server components. Deployment of this large-grained object may include distributing subcomponents across multiple heterogeneous computing resources in dispersed locations. Thus, an application designed on one processor is scattered across a network at run time.

Requirements for Capturing Business Object Benefits

Rapid deployment of a Business Process Architecture is the key to return on investment in object technology. This will not happen unless the Business Object development environment supports:

- Engineering from design (not hacking code)

- Standard OOAD methodologies

- Automated generation of code for standardized languages and interfaces

- Interoperability of Business Objects across domains through standardization of Business Object infrastructure to support plug and play components

Scalability of a Business Object Architecture is a requirement for putting mission-critical systems into production. The Architecture must support:

- Recursively nested components that scale to any size

- Distribution of these components across heterogeneous networked systems

Reusability of Business Object Components is essential to achieving reduced cycle time. The Business Object Architecture must support:

- Continuous Business Process Reengineering

- Controlled complexity through Business Components

- Code changes reflected back into design environment so that current design, documentation, and code can be continuously captured in an evolving object model.

- Legacy system connectivity so that older systems can be encapsulated as a Business Object Components.

Tools and methodologies for building distributed Business Objects are now emerging in new advanced application development tools. The ability of object-oriented software tool vendors to support robust development environments for design, assembly, and reuse of Business Objects is now enabling more widespread use of a Business Object Architecture in corporate development environments.

The Need for a Business Object Component Infrastructure

In 1986, Brad Cox[7] argued that software objects could be produced like integrated circuits and capture the benefits of Moore's law - the number of components on a silicon integrated chip doubles every year. By analogy, software productivity should double every year as off-the-shelf, plug compatible, software components increase in functionality.

The promise of object-technology has not been achieved during the last decade due the following factors:

- Productivity - Software productivity has declined on the average in the U.S. by 13% since 1993. However, the difference between productive and non-productive developments groups

---

[7] Cox, Brad. *Object-Oriented Programming: An Evolutionary Approach.* Addison-Wesley, 1986, p. 26.

has widened from 4:1 in 1990, to 600:1 in 1995.[8] Some organizations are making progress, most are falling farther behind.

- Reuse - The key to increased productivity is achieving 80% reuse of prebuilt objects. The average reuse in the industry is 20% for Smalltalk, less for other object-oriented languages. This is because most developers are using antiquated hand coding methods. Enhancing productivity requires that coding be automated.

- Automation - A good object-oriented design tool can generate 80% of the code for an application and reengineer existing code back into design.[9] Less than 10% of object-oriented developers were using these tools in 1995.

- Plug and Play Components - The only widely used plug and play components in recent years are VBX components for Visual Basic.[10] Plug and play components cannot exist without industry standards for component design. The two standards that exist today are OLE 2.0 (a defacto standard) and OMG CORBA 2.0 (inadequate for specification of design of interoperable components). IBM's DSOM is a CORBA implementation that could become an Object Management Group (OMG) standard. OMG BOMSIG and ANSI X3H7 Object Information Management are two committees working on standardization of a Business Object infrastructure based on OLE/CORBA integration.

- Component Market - Since component standards do not exist, no component market exists today. With the release of Windows 95, VBX vendors are converting products into OCX components which comply with Microsoft's OLE 2.0 specification. In 1996, a component market for OLE components will begin to emerge.

> *"Object technology failed to deliver on the promise of reuse. Visual Basic's custom controls succeeded. What role will object-oriented programming play in the component-software revolution that's now finally under way?"* John Udell, Byte Cover Story, May, 1994.

Developers of business information systems are beginning to take advantage of building applications with OLE components. At Object World in San Francisco, Allied Signal won the Computerworld Award for best object-oriented application of 1995.[11] They reengineered the Supply Management Business Process that took 52 steps to purchase a single part, so it now requires only three steps to complete the same transaction. The old process required seven people and took nine weeks to produce an approved purchase order. The new Supply Managment Specialist Tool (SMST), developed with the Object Studio[12] advanced development environment, allows one person to complete the same process in nine minutes for established suppliers with long-term agreements in place. In the case of new suppliers, where a Request For Quote (RFQ) is required, the process takes nine days.

---

[8] Yourdon, Ed. Productivity Metrics. *Ed Yourdon's Guerrilla Programmer 2:7* (Jul), 1995, p 7.

[9] VMARK Software. Object Studio Product Overview. VMARK Software, 1995 (http:/www.vmark.com/).

[10] Udell, John. Componentware. Byte, May, 1994. (http://www.byte.com/art/9405/sec5/art1.htm)

[11] VMARK Software. Allied Signal Company wins the Computerworld Object Application Award at Object World. Press Release, 21 August 1995. (http://www.vmark.com/whatsnew/presrel11.html)

[12] VMARK Software. Object Studio Product Literature, 1995. (http://www.vmark.com/products/objstud/objstud.html)

In this example, cycle time of the process is reduced 2400:1 for established suppliers, and 5:1 for new suppliers. Cost reduction is operational staff is 7:1. The impact of improvement in business efficiency leading to greater customer satisfaction and resulting market share is far greater than any reduced costs in operations overhead or development time and is the major motivator for the use of Business Object design tools to assure success of Business Process reengineering practice.

By 1997, it will be possible to buy 50% of an application as off-the-shelf components, effectively doubling productivity. By 1998, early adopters will be buying 50% of the application as external components and reusing internally generated components for another 25% of the application, effectively doubling productivity on an annual basis, and beginning to comply with Moore's law for IC chip design. Brad Cox's vision of software as IC chips will begin to be realized.

Conclusion

Corporations that take advantage of Business Object Architectures will significantly shorten product cycles. Consulting groups that use Business Objects will significantly underbid their competition and deliver new systems on time and under budget. Because a Business Object Architecture will allow software to change as rapidly as the underlying business processes, corporate viability will be enhanced by early implementation. Laggards will be easily outmaneuvered in the marketplace by enterprises already embarked on large-scale implementation of global distributed object systems.

The OMG Business Object Facility and the OMG Business Object

Oliver Sims

email: olivers@cix.compulink.co.uk

Abstract. This paper discusses some important implications of the OMG Request for Proposal (RFP) for "Common Business Objects". In particular the general "shape" of the run-time business objects, and the Business Object Facility which enables and supports them. Before discussing implications, the paper expands on two concepts which are fundamental to the RFP objectives. These are "Interoperability" and "Simplicity".

Introduction

In January 1996, the OMG issued a Request for Proposal (RFP) for "Common Business Objects" and for a "Business Object Facility". This is one of the first OMG RFPs to address explicitly the application developer and end user. The Business Object Facility (BOF) takes a "top-down" view, looking at the needs of the user and application developer, rather than the previously normal "bottom-up" approach, aimed at the infrastructure builders' needs. The BOF has two major objectives:

- Enable **interoperability** of independently-developed business objects as "plug-and-play" components of the information system
- Provide **simplicity** in the development, deployment, maintenance and use of business objects for application developers and users.

An additional objective of the RFP is that there should be a direct correspondence, in understandable business terms, between the business model and the run-time business objects[1] which are components of the information system.

The issues of interoperability and simplicity are discussed below.

Interoperability

The RFP talks of both "plug-and-play" and of "interoperability". These two are not synonyms. Let's deal with "plug-and-play" first.

Plug-and-Play

"Plug-and-play" means the ability to introduce a business object into a run-time environment so that an end user (or systems manager) can make use of it for some business purpose without any intervention being required by IT professionals. This process is sometimes known as

---

[1] The RFP defines the term "application component" to mean an object implementation that is the run-time manifestation of a business object. The term "business object" is used in the RFP as a synonym for "application component", and to refer to a design/modelling construct. In this paper, the term "business object" is used to denote both the run-time information system software object, and the design/modelling-time construct. This will, I hope, avoid confusion between an application component which really means a business object, and an application component as something a developer uses to build something else, but which is in no sense a plug-and-play thing of direct use to end users.

"composition", or, of course, "installation".

Installation ("plugging-in") of the business object must assume no compilation or linkage step, merely a very simple installation process, ideally requiring only base operating system facilities, into a running environment.

While plug-and-play implies that the object plugged in will be able to "play" (i.e. work), it does not necessarily imply interoperability - that is, does not imply that it will be able to interact effectively with other plug-and-play business objects.

Interoperability

"Interoperability" means that a newly plugged-in business object can be used (perhaps by an end user) in conjunction with, and interacting with, other business objects, such that their interaction performs some function useful for the business.

Since the developers of those business objects can never know with what other objects their products may be used, then such interaction must be able to be ad-hoc - that is, unplanned and unforeseen by developers. This is sometimes called "ad-hoc integration".

Interoperability introduces an important philosophical point. In general, when components (in our case, business objects) are to be integrated, there are two general approaches - or philosophies - relating to the process of integration:

- Optimistic - it is assumed that the business objects will interact as required, and if they don't, then it can be easily fixed
- Pessimistic - it is assumed that the business objects will not interact successfully, and therefore a "fix" process must firstly be executed - even when it is not required.

I much prefer the optimistic approach. While the pessimistic approach is more likely to identify potential problems up-front, it is also likely to impose increasingly lengthy procedures before anyone can plug and play and interoperate. In real-world terms, this would be like forcing someone to buy a micrometer in order to measure the precise diameter of a spark plug before being allowed to fit it. Sounds a bit dictatorial, doesn't it? I am strongly of the opinion that should the OMG adopt a pessimistic approach, then plug-and-play, not to mention interoperability, will be lost in a general move towards demanding sophisticated integration tools that only developers can hope to use. Such an approach would be much easier for the implementors of a Business Object Facility; however, it would kill the very objectives of the RFP.

Having said that, it is well worth noting that anyone who wishes to do so can fairly easily impose a pessimistic approach onto the optimistic one. The reverse is not true. If the Business Object Facility were to provide for plug-and-play *only* through some "fit-and-pre-test" tools, then one could only move towards some optimism by introducing an *additional* layer of tools, which "drove" the underlying tools based on some non-standard set of assumptions.

This paper assumes an optimistic philosophy for both plug-and-play and interoperation.

Simplicity

By "Simplicity", the RFP means hiding software technology complexities so that the application developer, whose skills lie in business solutions (as opposed to the software technologist who is skilled in system programming), can viably *implement* business objects. In turn, the business objects themselves should be plug-and-play interoperable components which an end user can use directly as parts of a business solution.

What *is* an OMG business object?

We know that a business object is something that exists; it is a cohesive lump of software in the run-time environment. Can we derive a more specific description than this?

An executable ...

The plug-and-play requirement means that the business object must be delivered as a separate executable - developed independently of other similar executables.

By "executable" I mean compiled and linked code - a binary - which, having been delivered by some developer and deployed into the Business Object Facility run-time environment, needs no other preparation before being executed or run. Examples of an executable are a Windows DLL or EXE file, or a Unix shared library member (again, a file).

Why do I rule out a specific language run-time environment, or perhaps a specific 4GL? Well, recollect that OMG standards and specifications deliberately do not pre-define any specific language. Although the RFP does not state this explicitly, it is nevertheless clear that business objects should be able to be built with any of the common languages in use today (or, hopefully, tomorrow!). That is, a developer of a business object should have a choice of languages in which to develop the business object. Hence the Business Object Facility should support language-neutrality; and hence it cannot itself be bounded by a specific language environment.

If the "executable" is written in an interpreted language, then an aspect of the language binding would be to provide a run-time layer which would map the Business Object Facility to the interpreter, and to the interpreted code. A 4GL could generate code, or intermediate interpreted code, to the required shape.

... of a specific "shape"

In order to plug the business object - the executable - into the Business Object Facility, then the business object must be of a known and standard software "shape". If it were not, then the receiving run-time system into which it is plugged - the Business Object Facility - could neither handle it, nor make it available to users and/or other business objects.

Implication 1: The Business Object is an independently-developed executable, and its software "shape" is defined by the Business Object Facility.

In my opinion, it is likely that this executable will be more easily handled as a dynamically-linkable entity, so that it can, if required, be run in the same address space (process) as other business objects. Assigning a separate address space for each object implementation seems to me to be sub-optimal, for a number of reasons (outside the scope of this paper).

Having looked at the implications of plug-and-play, let's now discuss interoperability - or ad-hoc interactions between separately-developed business objects.

Loose binding ...

Consider two separately-developed business objects. Interaction between the two must be able to be completely ad-hoc - that is, without that interaction necessarily having been planned for or even foreseen by the developers of the business objects. In other words, two business objects might meet for the very first time when a message is sent from one to the other. Before that event, such interaction may well never have been planned for - or even imagined - by any developer.

Clearly, for interaction to be effective, both business objects must embody some common concepts. That is, each developer of the interacting objects must have "agreed" to use the same concepts - but without their previously having agreed to agree! This must imply a common understanding of concepts, both those to do with the basic behaviour of objects (such as "Set" an attribute to some value), and those to do with the domain of interaction (such as "accounting" or "medical records"). Basic behaviour might be defined by the Business Object Facility. Let us assume that domain-specific behaviour and concepts are defined in some standard and publicly-available form. Within an organisation, one can see how this might be achieved; for inter-organisation commonality, we enter the realm of Common Business Objects (the other part of the RFP) - and of possible future domain-specific business object models.

Now if ad-hoc interaction depended on both developers using firstly the same IDL, and secondly the same version of that IDL, then the chances of successful interaction would be small. This is because IDL defines binding between objects in terms of computational detail such as data types, structures and sequences. For example, a user may know that two objects both embody the concept of "age". However, if the run-time interaction between objects is in terms of an integer by one object and a string by the other, then not only would there be a type mismatch, but there would also be confusion as to which of several integers (or strings) passed in a message is the one encoding a value for the concept "age".

What is required is a much looser kind of binding - one that can be done for the first time ever at message time, where the developers cannot be expected to hit on identical computational details.

Let's test this assertion. IDL can be said to provide a kind of distributed linkage editor, so that type-checking etc. can be done at build time - without actually having all components of the executable present to be bound, and without having entry points unambiguously identified. Now ask of any IS Manager whether he/she would like all the organisations' applications to be link-edited together, an implication being that a change in any interface may require re-linking a substantial number of parts. You would be thrown out of the office! As IS departments and business solutions move towards inter-application interaction, most implementors find that they need a much looser binding than can be achieved with IDL as it is currently used.

Implication 2: Business object interoperability requires loose binding.

What we're saying here is that business objects should not be glued or welded together; they should be clipped or blue-tacked together. The lower-level technology objects used by middleware are the ones that need to be glued or welded together with much tighter binding. Indeed, CORBA and the current OMGfacilities and OMGservices are ideally-suited to such use.

It might be thought that an implication of this discussion is that IDL needs to be changed, or significantly enhanced. I do not believe this is necessarily the case. However, further examination of this topic is beyond the scope of this paper.

What we now need to touch on is this: how do we in general provide loose binding - or binding on concept only?

... with "Semantic" data

Loose binding is provided by minimising the "surface area" (Cox, p.16), or number of separate elements that the developer needs to consider at build time. What is required is to provide binding at the highest possible level - preferably at the level of the *semantics* of the interaction. It should not matter which computational details (type or sequence of data items) developers choose; the thing they must share is a common understanding of the concepts being communicated.

Common understanding alone, however, is not a sufficient condition for ad-hoc interoperability. The concepts must be encoded in some way so that at run-time each object can recognise the other's concepts. This seems to imply strongly that the semantics of interactions, and of data passed between business objects during those interactions, must be able to be encoded within message data. This can be done by having all message data in a self-describing form, where labels (metadata) for data values are passed together with the values. In fact, in a given message between business objects, the various items of self-defined data can be placed into an object - a "semantic data object". The business object message then contains, as its message data, an instance of the "semantic data" class.

Such an approach can also handle type mismatches, by performing automatic type conversions where required (this can give problems, but experience - with the "Newi" product from SSA Object technology - has shown that the benefits significantly outweigh the disadvantages).

Semantic interaction also has the great advantage that it can correspond directly to business object models. Thus some attribute label "CustomerName" in the model also flows in encoded form at run-time in object interaction.

Implication 3: Message data should be encoded semantically.

Here is a simple example of the use of semantic data. Suppose I wanted to send a message to some object, and to send it a customer name, a customer number and a credit limit. Without semantic data, I might send the following structure (again, in pseudocode):

```
Structure:
    string  30
    string  7
    integer
End-Structure
```

This would be encoded in the message at run-time something like this:

```
"Smith & Co.              AB12345000150000"
```

To make sense of this, the recipient would have to share with me the following pieces on knowledge, none of which appears in the message:

- the sequence of items (name, then customer number, then credit limit)
- the size of each item
- the type of each item in the structure
- the length of any variable-length items in the structure
- what each item actually *means* (its semantic value)

If I were to encode this same information as semantic data, then this is what might appear in the message I send:

```
"CustName=Smith & Co. | AccountNo=AB12345 | CreditLimit=1500.00"
```

To make sense of this, the recipient would have to share with me only one piece on knowledge which does not appear in the message:

- The meaning of the labels "CustName", "AccountNo" and "CreditLimit"

Types, data lengths and data structure can be hidden from the developer by the semantic data class. Methods provided by this class would enable the recipient to "pull out" any one data item independently of others. So to get the Customer Name, the recipient might code (in the invoked method of the receiving business object) something like this:

```
name = SemanticDataObjectReceived<--Get("CustName")
```

There is clearly more to semantic data than we can deal with in this paper. For example, homonym and synonym handling must be able to be applied without touching the delivered business objects themselves. Nevertheless, the above shows in outline how semantic data can deliver significantly loose binding to business objects by focusing surface area on the *semantics* of the interaction. Furthermore, and importantly, experience has shown that building and parsing semantic data can be made viable for the application developer.

We have concluded that the business object is an executable. We now go on to consider what it looks like to the developer.

What does a business object look like?

Hiding complexity

A major objective of the RFP is that a business object should be able to be built by an IS developer who is focusing on business logic rather than on software technicalities such as threads, memory management, multiple different system-level APIs, etc. (We might dare to go further, and to say that, with the appropriate tools, a business object should be able to be built by an ambitious end user.) Meeting this objective implies that the significant amounts of complexity inherent in writing business solutions directly on existing interfaces provided by the ORB, CORBAfacilities and CORBAservices must be hidden.

Why hide rather than simplify? The reason is this. Although it is generally possible to simplify the syntax of lower-level software complexities, it is seldom possible to simplify the semantics as well - to hide the range of knowledge needed to drive the simplified syntax. And it is in the semantics that the complexity typically lies.

Hiding complexity is done by imposing constraints on the programmer's freedom of choice.   An ideal approach is to hide complexities through constraints, but without preventing a software technologist to move, with clever programming, outside those constraints.

A good way of imposing constraints is to provide a specific "programmer's model" - a specific "shape" of code. This is not at all a new idea; it is what teleprocessing monitors do - they define the shape of a transaction program, and so hide significant computational software complexities. After all, the programmer cannot expect to build a monolithic application of any shape and have it be both simple to build *and* be plug-and-play and interoperable!

However, we have already said that the business object must be an executable of a specific "shape" in order to be plug-and-play. This might seem to be serendipitous. On the other hand, it might be evidence that we are on the right track - two different requirements lead to similar conclusions. So let's define a shape that can hide complexity.

Implication 4: The business object must be of a specific technical software shape.

Also, remember that one of the requirements mentioned in the RFP is that the developer should create a unit of delivery which maps as closely as possible to the business object concept defined in the business object model.

The conclusion is that the unit of delivery should itself be an object - or more precisely, the implementation of a class.

Implication 5: The business object should be the implementation of a class.

A further constraint is that the developer should be able to use a variety of languages, including perhaps procedural and scripting languages, to build the business object implementation. This means that such things as inheritance, handling multiple instances, providing space for instance data, etc., cannot be left to an OO language. That is, these things must be handled *outside* the unit of delivery.

Implication 6: The business object must be language-neutral

Finally, by the nature of plug-and-play business objects, the developer *cannot* know about such things as when his/her code must be loaded, which thread it will run in (if at all), how many instances of his/her class are created - and hence how much memory is required for instance data, etc. For this reason, the loading and invocation of executables, memory management, thread management, instance management, communications management, blocking issues, etc. are all things which must or should also be placed *outside* the code implementing the business object executable.

That so much must be removed from the concern of the developer is a welcome conclusion. For such things *should* be of no concern to the developer, if we are to succeed in hiding complexity. In addition, by defining what factors should not be handled by the developer, we gain some purchase on the question of what the Business Object Facility itself must or should handle.

The Business Object programmer's model

We are now almost ready to suggest a possible programmer's model - the "shape" of the executable - of a business object. There is one other consideration which arises from the language-neutrality and loose binding implications. That is, method resolution cannot be done by executables having multiple entry points, since some languages do not support this. There are various ways to overcome this constraint, including a call-back registration approach (however this again limits the language choice). The simplest way of dealing with this constraint is, I believe, for each unit of delivery to have a single well-known entry point, and for the developer to handle method resolution *within* the business object implementation.

With this, and other factors discussed above in mind, then a "shape" of business object implementation might look something like this (shown in procedural pseudocode; OO pseudocode could also be used):

```
Start (business object invoked when a message arrives)

    Determine message

    StartCase handle message

        Case message = "Query"
            code for responding to a query
            invoke superclass
            return

        Case message = "Commit"
            Self "Query"
            Send result of query to database object
            return

        etc.

    End Case

    invoke superclass

End
```

Figure 1

The Business Object Facility could map all events of interest to business objects to incoming messages. Such uniformity assists with the simplicity objective.

This shape of code can be compiled and linked, and the resulting executable assigned a position in a class hierarchy. Interpreted languages can also be managed. When a message is sent to an instance of the class for which this code is the implementation, then the code is loaded, and the message passed to it. The message itself might itself be a small-grained object whose attributes might include:

·Message Name
·Id of target business object
·Id of invoking business object
·Semantic data object sent by invoking object
·Semantic data object for data to be returned from invoked object

Instance data for the specific instance could be handed to the developer automatically. For example, a buffer containing the instance data could be handed to the implementation at the same time it is invoked by a message.

Interaction between business objects

In the pseudocode above, we see the object sending messages both to itself, to its superclass and to another object. This is one area where, in real business systems, significant complexities lie in wait to trap the unwary. And in turn, this is an excellent area to exemplify hiding complexity. Indeed, a major advantage of the shape of code shown is that it provides a highly suitable vehicle for hiding complexity.

Consider, for example, an asynchronous messaging capability. This would be tailored to the application developer, in a top-down way. The first conclusion would be that the asynchronous message is asynchronous *with respect to the developer's code*. The major problem with this is how to provide the response to the developer, without him or her having to engage in call-backs, thread management, or other complexities. We may determine, for example, that the application programmer would like to be able to do the following:

    Write a single statement which causes a message to be sent asynchronously

•Define the message he/she wants to be returned with the response
•Have that response message delivered to him/her as all other messages are

From this, we might say that the programmer should be able to write something like the following, where in the method "Search" the message "DoSearch" is sent as an asynchronous message to business object X, and the result is requested as message "DoneIt":

```
Start (business object invoked when a message arrives)

    StartCase handle message
        ...
        Case message = "Search"
            ...
            SendAsync to X, "DoSearch", response message = "DoneIt"
            ...

        Case message = "DoneIt"
            handle result of "DoSearch"
            ...

    End Case

    invoke superclass

End
```

Figure 2

Experience with business objects to date has shown that while asynchronous messaging (from the point of view of the application programmer) should be used with caution to avoid getting into FSM (Finite State Machine) coding complexities, its use is sometimes necessary in real business systems. Normally, however, the programmer would prefer to use synchronous messaging, perhaps something like this (note that for clarity, handling of message data is not shown in Figs 2 or 3):

```
Start (business object invoked when a message arrives)

    StartCase handle message

        Case message = "Search"
            ...
            SendSync to X, "DoSearch"
            handle result of "DoSearch"
            ...

        etc.

    End Case

    invoke superclass

End
```

Figure 3

In both the above cases, there is no inherent computational complexity visible to the programmer. However, business object messaging of the kind described above does imply complex issues of blocking, re-entrancy and thread management (and of the underlying communications layer). These issues, and their resolution, can be hidden from the application developer through use of a specific programmer's model of the general shape described above. The complexities are exported to (handled by) the Business Object Facility, which defines and supports the programmer's model - the "shape" of the business object.

For example, in addition to the issues mentioned, the BOF would define "asynchronous" from the point of view of the developer; for example, "The developer will not receive a response message until he/she has completed the method in which an asynchronous message was issued".

Again, consider the recipient of a message; the developer should not have to be concerned as to whether his business object was invoked with an asynchronous or synchronous message. The programmer's model shown can enable the BOF to provide a model of invocation which could hide any differences from the developer. One of the things that makes this feasible is the use of semantic data objects for all message data. Thus the BOF, if it needs to handle message data on behalf of a business object, will always see just one type - a "semantic data object".

Mapping to the business model

As mentioned at the start of the paper, a major objective of the RFP is to provide a direct correspondence between a business object defined in an object model and a defined component in the information system. The programmer's model above, being itself a class which is enabled to live and breathe by the Business Object Facility, clearly provides a basis for this objective to be achieved.

Business object models will not infrequently define things other than class attributes and behaviour. They will also define such things as superclasses and relationships. Again, many facilities such as transaction support, business object name spaces, events, "views" of objects and roles will be required. It is worth noting that the Business Object Facility could provide frameworks to handle such things. Such frameworks could feasibly be built using the business object programmer's model, and using the Business Object Facility as their run-time environment. Of course, these frameworks would in many cases wrap specific uses of the CORBAfacilities and CORBAservices. This may be a useful way to hide the complexities inherent in some of those facilities and services.

Finally, the question of dependencies must be addressed. If plug-and-play components have too many dependencies on other pieces of software, and those dependencies have other dependencies, then the chance of achieving true plug-and-play is significantly reduced. The business object model described, by defining a clear first-cut design rule for the granularity and content of executables, can help significantly with handling this problem.

Summary of implications

Here is a summary of the various implications found in the course of the paper:

The Business Object is an independently-developed executable, and its software "shape" is defined by the Business Object Facility.

Business object interoperability requires loose binding.

Message data should be encoded semantically.

The business object must be of a specific technical software shape.

The business object should be the implementation of a class.

The business object must be language-neutral

Areas of standardisation

To enable the above implementation shape of business objects, the Business Object Facility would probably have to define standards in six general areas:

Technical description of the executable

Interfaces to supporting/enabling CORBA objects

Message structure (CORBA says nothing about this)

Precise way in which the BOF uses CORBA and CORBAservices and CORBAfacilities

Management of class hierarchies

Specific interfaces for tools, and support for ("hooks") underlying systems management and security facilities (these may be subsumed in the above five areas)

An immediate question is, can the above general approach be implemented without significant extensions to CORBA? I believe the answer is yes. In this paper, I cannot expand significantly on this answer. Suffice to say that I believe there is a very natural way to see a business object implementation as a CORBA object - and provide the characteristics described above.

References

Cox: "Object-Oriented Programming - an evolutionary approach", Brad J. Cox & Andrew J. Novobilski, Addison-Wesley 1991

OMG   Document CF/96-01-04, "Common Facilities RFP-4, Common Business Objects and Business Object Facility"

An Architecture Framework:
From Business Strategies to Implementation

William F. Hertha, Jim E. Bennett, Frank J. Post, Ian M. Page

Architecture Services,
Canadian Imperial Bank of Commerce
901 King St. W. 7th Floor, Commerce Court Postal Station 'A'
Toronto, Ontario, Canada
E-mail: bhertha@mtnlake.com Fax: 1 416 980 3099

ABSTRACT. *Business systems architects and their clients increasingly suffer from information overload. To help businesses to partition and relate the kinds of architecture information they must build and share, we propose a framework consisting of three related models, each incorporating four tiers of subject matter connected by use cases.*

KEY WORDS: *Architecture Framework Strategy Process Component*

---

1.   Introduction

Preparing an architecture for large business systems is never an easy task, and in today's business climate it is made more difficult than ever. The expectations are higher, and the alternatives are wider. There is a great amount and variety of information to absorb.

As Figure 1 illustrates, this paper will explore a four-tier three-model framework which we feel can help to organise and communicate this information.

	Models		
	Reference Model	EndState Model	Deployable Model
Strategy Tier			
Process Tier			
Application Object Tier			
Technology Tier			

Figure 1: Architecture Framework

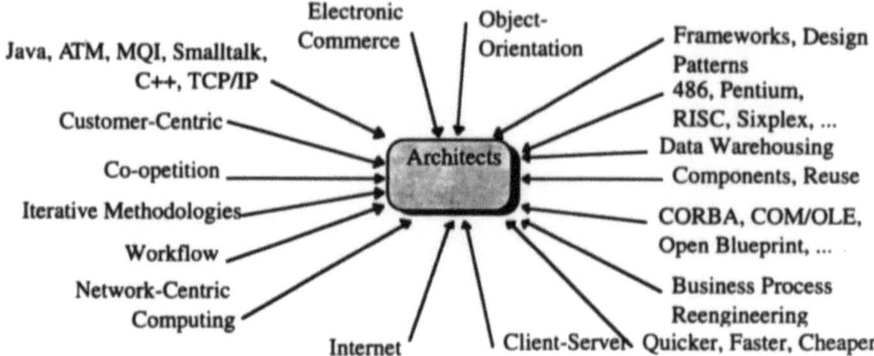

Figure 2: Challenges for Architects

As Figure 2 shows, the problem of preparing an architecture has become large and complex. Even its scope is not universally agreed. An architecture cannot be created by a small group of people isolated from the business that needs the technology nor from the people that have to apply it to solve business problems. It requires the involvement of many people, from several disciplines.

Business clients need to be involved so that technology is applied to the areas where it can provide the most value. At the other end of the spectrum, technologists need to be involved because they understand what works, and what does not.

Mark Fox [Fox95] says *"Many artifacts, including those produced by the project's participating corporations, are so complex that designs require the efforts of many engineers. This means that the artifact must be functionally and/or physically decomposed, and the pieces divided amongst groups of engineers. The major issue in 'Design-in-the-Large' is how to achieve high levels of collaboration among engineers. That is, how each engineer's design task can be managed so that it integrates well with the results of others."*

The experience of many business systems architects suggests that we need ...

- .. A way to accumulate, organise and communicate information. A project of this magnitude and duration will result in a vast amount of information and knowledge being generated. Participants will come and go. The information has to grow and evolve even though the contributors may change.

- .. A common vision and language. If we are to muster an army of individuals to realise an objective, they all have to be clear what that objective is, the more so because of the different backgrounds, different skill sets, and different understandings of terms and concepts.

- .. The ability to address sufficient scope. Many of the architectures currently proposed focus only on a subset of the domain, mostly the technology infrastructure -- the hardware, software, tools -- and only to a lesser degree are applications or processes considered. Rarely do we see any discussion on the broader systems problem *and* how it relates to the business processes that must employ the technology and the business strategies that caused those business processes to come into being.

- .. To partition the problem domain, especially if we are enlarging the scope.

- .. To assign clear responsibility for each task resulting from our partitioning.

- .. To match the right skills to each task resulting from our partitioning. If we are to expand our view to integrate technical solutions into the business solutions, we need to distinguish these tasks, and apply business skills, business process engineering skills, analytical skills and pure technology skills, where appropriate. Applying the wrong skills to a task can lead to disastrous results.

- .. To relate the solutions to the business need. The solutions that are prepared must be shown to be tied to the problem they are intended to resolve. Too frequently we hear the phrase "a solution looking for a problem."

- .. To be selective about what we make flexible, as building flexible solutions costs time and money. Too often we blindly overpay for flexibility in the hope that the solution will later be tied to some unknown or unclearly specified needs, rather than understanding the needs in the first place.

- .. To be able to accommodate our existing systems. We cannot assume that the business can afford to replace all the existing systems, and even if they could, the implied risks and challenges makes such considerations infeasible.

- .. To be able to adapt to change, whether it comes from the business or from the availability of new technologies. The architecture we create cannot impose a static framework, never able to accommodate change. We must be able to incorporate new business strategies and new technologies with minimal impact.

2.   Three Models, Four Tiers

What we propose is an approach which relates three models:

1. The first defines an architecture Reference Model (RM): the Reference Model is actually a meta-architecture which identifies and relates the *kinds* of information we expect to include in our EndState architecture. We start with a Reference Model because there is no universal definition of an architecture, and we need common concepts and language which multiple groups of people can work with.

2. The second model is the EndState Model (EM): the model that we would like to implement in a specific business. We propose a component-based approach where the EndState defines specific components within each tier, based on the kinds suggested in the Reference Model.

3. The third model is the Deployable Model (DM): the actual set of production systems which satisfy the EndState component specifications, to a greater or lesser degree.

Each model has the same four tiers:

1. Strategies Tier (ST). The business prepares its strategies: its principles, its objectives for quality, cost, scale, and performance, the events it wants to respond to, the results it wants to deliver.

2. Processes Tier (PT). The strategies are implemented as business processes --workflows and procedures people follow in responding to events.

3. Application Objects Tier (OT). Applications, which are assembled from Object-based Components, to supply the required process support .

4. Technology Tier (TT). The hardware, technical software, and systems management put in place to run the applications.

3. Tier Contents and Relationships

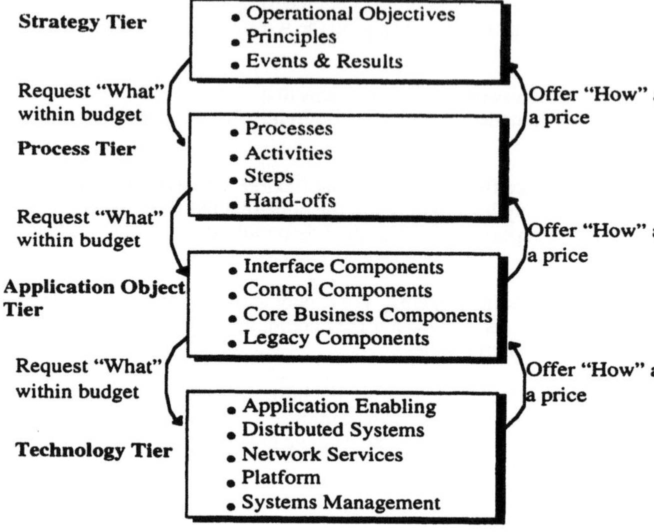

Figure 3: The Reference Model

shown, we cannot show that we are satisfying a business need. If we cannot show traceability to value, then we are left with the impression of doing technology for its own sake.

3.1 Relationships Between Tiers

Figure shows between each tier there is an explicit "what-how" relationship. The strategies state "what" business processes must accomplish, and conversely, a business process represents "how" a business strategy is implemented. This "what/how" relationship continues through the complete model, enabling clear communication between the tiers of "what" requirements and of "how" counter-offers to service those requirements, as shown in Figure 1: Relationship between Tiers.

We extend Jacobson's notion of use cases [Jac92] as the mechanism for communicating between the tiers. Each inter-tier use case specification identifies a set of inputs, expected results, relevant principles, operational objectives and size/volume metrics. Each such specification identifies specific actions on one or more components in the adjacent tier, and is the basis for accountability and traceability.

As for the components, we combine the notions promoted by Wirfs-Brock et al [Wir90] and the Object Management Group [OMG.93.12.29] to say a component represents a distinct set of responsibilities, which are visible through a set of interfaces, enabling developers to design to the interface, not the implementation. In this way, each component will express *what* it is capable of doing, in the same terms as the component expressing the need. This allows us to communicate on a common "what" footing among components, regardless of whether they are resident in the same or adjacent tiers.

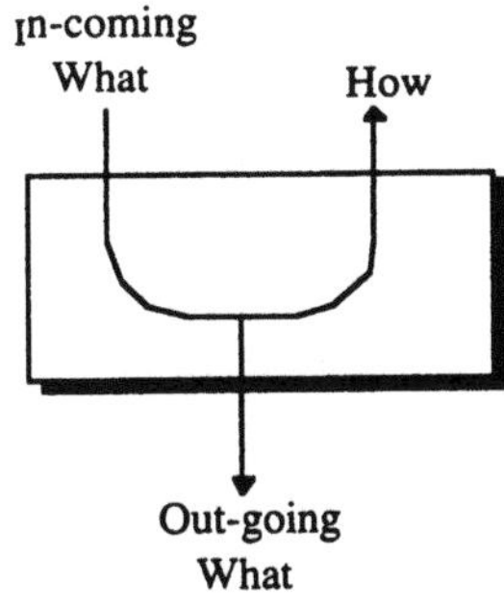

**Figure 1: Relationship
between Tiers**

However the incoming "what" expressed to a component may not be the same as the "out-going what" it will express to other components.

For example, it may be possible to implement a business strategy completely with manual processes. But if parts of the solution are to be automated, then we must refine the "what" incoming to the Process Tier to a "what" outgoing to the Application Object Tier. For example, Operational Objectives stated in the strategy may define end-to-end timing requirements of the implementing business process, while Operational Objectives stated to supporting application tier are focused to the activity being supported such as specific response time requirements.

3.2. *Strategy Tier*

Within the Strategy Tier, high-level business goals are formed into the specific components of interest to other tiers: events and their corresponding results, operational objectives, and principles.

Events define what the business is expected to respond to. Results state the expected outcome. Operational Objectives state quality, quantity, time, and cost objectives for the way that business processes will respond to specific events. Principles provide overriding factors, such as company policy, legislation, etc. Together, this information defines a use case for a business process.

3.3. *Process Tier*

As shown in Figure processes are defined by partitioning them into activities and steps and showing hand-offs between activities. We define *Activity* as the unit of accountability within a process. Activities may be manually executed and hand-offs may be manually forwarded, or there may be automated tools. Activities and Hand-offs are among the components of this tier.

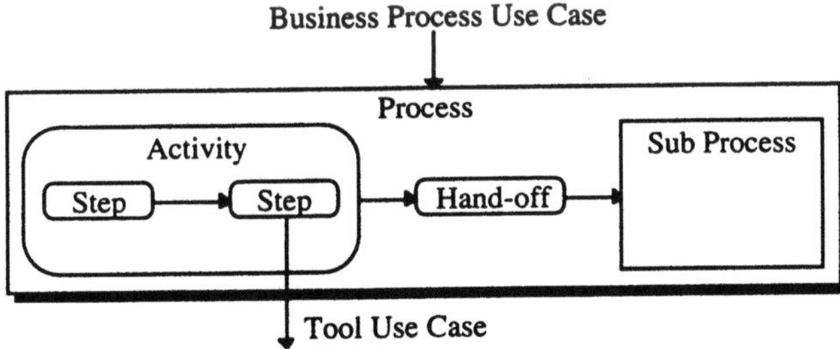

Figure 5:   Process Tier

3.4. *Application Object Tier*

As shown in Figure 6, one useful way of classifying the components of this Tier is the ICE model [Jac92], made up of Interface, Control (integrity glue), and Entity (core business and legacy system) component types. Another way might be by source: general, industry-specific,

52

vendor, or custom. The Object Management Group, through some of its special interest groups, is addressing the problem from this perspective [BOM95].

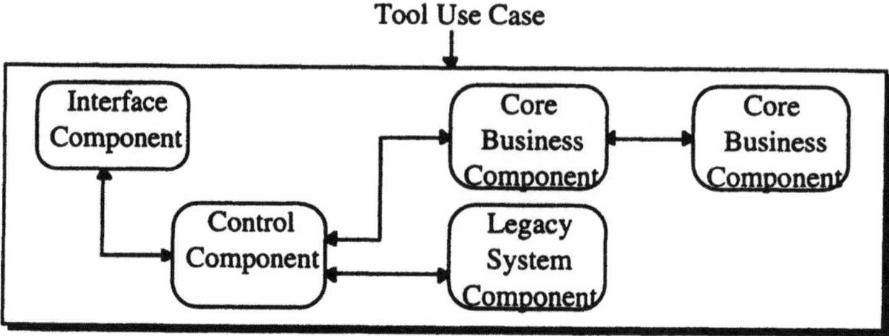

Figure 6: Application Object Tier

The Tool Use Cases (Figure 6) define the requirements of responsibility-based Application Components. In fact, a use case from any one activity represents a subset of the requirements of an application component. The full set of requirements of a particular component is realised by combining the requirements of all use cases which employ it. Collaboration among components defines further "interior" use cases.

3.5. Technology Tier

The Components of this tier might be classified (following IBM's Open Blueprint [IBM95]) into the following component types: Application Enabling Services, Distributed Systems Services, Network Services, Platform Services and Systems Management, as shown in Figure 7. The Common Object Request Broker Architecture (CORBA) [OMG.93.12.29] and other sources might have different schemes.

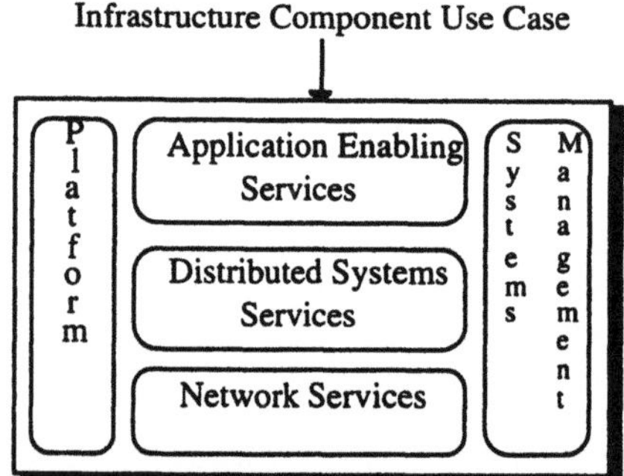

Figure 7: Technology Tier

Application Enabling Services support "applications" with regard to presentation, persistence, transaction monitoring, etc. Distributed Systems Services enable the distribution of function and data, while Network Services provide the communications infrastructure. The Platform Component includes operating systems and hardware, while Systems Management provides the necessary tools to manage the infrastructure.

Interactions with the Technology can occur explicitly (an application or technology component may request services), or implicitly (resources, such as CPU time and bandwidth are consumed in passing). At least in the explicit case we can again employ the use case approach, specifying the inputs and expected results, operational objectives, and principles.

4.   Model Contents and Relationships

4.1.   Relationship Between Models

Figure 8 shows bi-directional relationships between the three models. Going from left to right, the Reference Model suggests the kinds of information to be collected and who might best define them. This in turn can suggest the definition of some specific EndState components that a particular business will need. And this in turn can suggest how this can be Deployed, now or in some future phase, to make the business operate as intended.

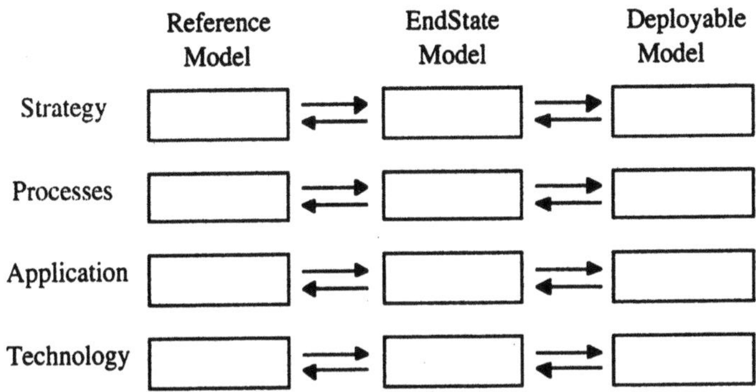

Figure 8: Relationship Between Models

Conversely, going from right to left, the functionality of existing implemented systems tells us what needs are currently being met, which implies generic EndState components to model the capability. The Reference Model might usefully frame the thinking about what sorts of components should contain that functionality, or conversely the need for new components may suggest ways in which the Reference Model is deficient.

4.2.   The Reference Model

The Reference Model defines the kinds of components that should be found in each of the four tiers. For example, we should include event definitions and result requirements in the Strategy Tier, activity and hand-off definitions in the Process Tier, methods and parts in the Application Object Tier, and operational objectives statements in every tier.

The Reference Model can be used in analysing a wide range of businesses; financial services, manufacturing, etc. It does not say what actual components apply to the analysis of a given business.

When a reference model is being prepared for a specific business, one could identify specific standards or guidelines to be used at each tier to guide the kinds of components to be included, such as OMG's CORBA or IBM's Open Blueprint.

4.3 . The EndState Model (EM)

With a defined Reference Model, we are now in a position to state what kinds of component should be included in each tier of the EndState Model of a specific business. The Reference Model might tell us that the Process Tier includes Activity components, and we might decide that we want a TakeCustomerOrder activity in our EM. Or the Reference Model may state the need for Core Business Components, but the definition of a Customer or Person or Organisation component is left to the EM.

4.4. *The Deployable Model (DM)*

We can now map EM components to deployable targets in each tier. If the EndState Model tells us that we want a TakeCustomerOrder activity, then in the DM we must deliver one or more standard implementations of that activity. Similarly, having defined a customer Core Business Component in the EM, we have to buy or build one or more objects or wrapped legacy systems to meet the specification. Likewise, having decided that the EM needs a Relational DBMS component, we have to pick deployable products.

5. Managing Change

Deployable components will often be deficient with respect to the EndState Model. For example, wrapped legacy application components may lack the inheritance required of true objects as well as some required functionality. Deployed strategies may fail to live up to some EndState principles. The so-called EndState may need to change. Therefore we need migration plans to more closely align the DM to the EM, or vice-versa.

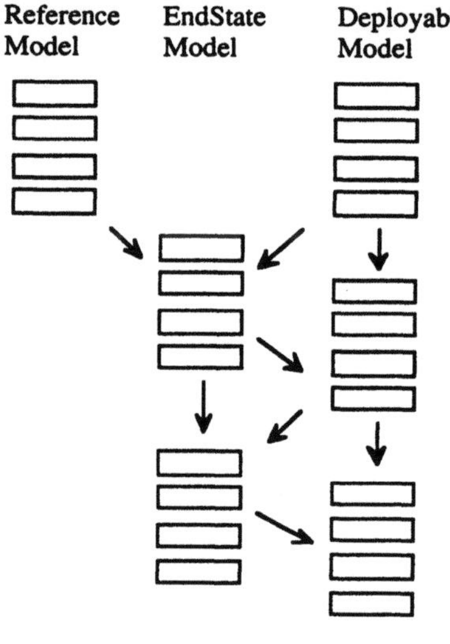

Figure shows a possible sequence of change and realignment of models.

We may begin by forming an EndState Model based on our Reference Model and the current Deployed Model. Then we may change Deployable Model to more closely align it with the EndState. At some point, we may change our EndState based on deployment experience, and then change the Deployable Model to match.

Change can be introduced for reasons other than alignment, ranging from changes in the Strategy to changes in the technology used to implement components. We can generalise this type of change as either a change in implementation (how) or a change in requirements (what). If we must realign component boundaries, we prefer to create new components for new functions, rather than redefining existing components for existing users. While changes in implementation may be isolated by encapsulation, changes in requirements may affect the boundaries of our components, thus affecting the EndState Model.

Figure 9: Change and Realignment

If we have built our components around natural and stable responsibilities, the functional model should be quite long-lived. But as Figure 10 shows, we may want component variants based on different operational objectives and possibly different operational interfaces. A new technology may sometimes suggest new components by highlighting EndState operational deficiencies. Clients of the component who are concerned only with functionality will see no difference.

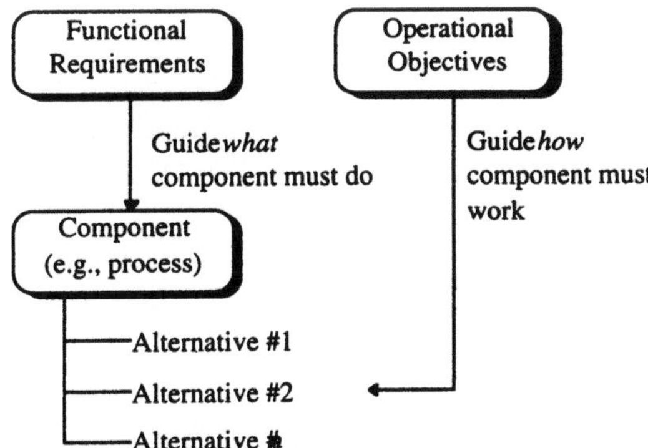

Figure 10: Functional Requirements versus Operational Objectives

6. Packages

Deployable implementations, whether bought or home-grown, may not map easily to the components defined in the EndState Model as a result of their packaging. We view a package as a set of component functions and parts and responsibilities, which may be grouped on some basis other than the EndState Architecture's component partitioning, such as pricing or installation cycle or buyer or builder.

Packaging may therefore cause us some problems. A new package may include an already implemented component. Or the package may contain a component only partially matching our definition (either functional requirements or operational objectives).

7. Areas of Further Research

7.1. *Accommodating Flexibility and Risk*

To handle an uncertain future, we often want to describe a family of requirements scenarios at each tier. We would probably pay a premium for solutions which require minimum time and cost to adapt when we change the request to one of the other scenarios. Should this be handled simply by developing a "how" offer for each scenario and comparing them, or can we devise more powerful techniques for handling families ?

7.2. *Concepts and Terminology*

Some industry groups are using terms such as Business Process and Business Component to refer only to application software elements. Our additional tiers extend these concepts. For example, we feel that Activities and Hand-offs are Business Components, though they are not software. We would like to find a common reference model over all four tiers.

7.3. *Separating Functional Requirements from Operational Objectives*

We need to further explore the difference between requirements and objectives. Our current approach is to distinguish Functional Requirements from Operating Objectives in each tier.

- Functional requirements direct *what* a component must do, what it must accomplish.

· Operational Objectives influence *how* the component is actually implemented.

Functional Requirements state the business needs in non technical, implementation-free terms. Operational Objectives, on the other hand, state goals which solutions are expected to meet or surpass, which are generally related to cost, time, skills necessary to execute a task, legislative requirements, etc. We use the term Business Requirement to encompass both Functional Requirements and Operational Objectives.

7.4. Identifying Events vs Processes

When is it best to recognise different events at the strategy level, and when is it better to merely distinguish different variants of "how" the event is handled ?

For example, in banking we could identify a withdraw-cash event, and state appropriate functional requirements. Objectives that might influence how the event is implemented could include: it must cost less than $0.25, it must be do-able directly by our customers, it must not take longer than 1 minute for the complete transaction, etc. However the same event could have a second set of objectives. For example, the above description may be appropriate for customers who use Automated Banking Machines, but a different set of objectives may be appropriate for those that use tellers.

From the Strategy perspective, should this be seen as one event or as different events? We can see the case for both, and therefore we need to better understand when the "how" should be "visible" and when it should be hidden as an implementation detail.

7.5 . How the Framework Facilitates Development Processes

Some development issues we hope to address with the proposed framework include:

· **Application design reviews** - We believe it may be easier to separate process and workflow logic from business component logic, and technology issues from business issues.

· **Package acquisition decisions** -We hope to get a clearer picture of both the fit with current requirements and the prospects for later reuse and recombination.

· **Business requirements gathering** -We would like to frame the discussion in terms of producing satisfaction for business events, in the belief that both the business and the three "how" tiers can find common ground there.

· **Technology upgrade business cases** -By following the suggested linkages, it should be easier to show how better technology positively affects the "good, quick, cheap" operational objectives of the strategy, process and application tiers.

· **Definition of use cases of various kinds** - Clarifying the relevant "client" tier should make it more straightforward to get a solid specification for a component in any "how" tier. For example, a component can be better specified by knowing the set of processes in which it will be invoked; a technology component can be better specified by knowing how component collaborations will use it. In fact, a component may be specified by a collection of such use cases, though we should never claim to know all the potential use cases.

· **Patterns and Frameworks** - The reference model needs to accommodate types of patterns and frameworks in each of the tiers of the EndState Model, but we have not yet worked out how best to do that. Our belief is that patterns will provide a standard way of documenting alternative general implementations. Such an inventory would help developers to plan, to find solutions with known costs and risks, and to communicate available solutions to their clients. This latter point would help us make clearer counter-offers as suggested earlier (see **Error! Reference source not found.**).

- **Reuse** - We believe that the kinds of reuse that deliver the highest leverage occur at the highest levels of design. But of course we would like to encourage developers to build for potential reuse at all levels, and we hope to do this by aiming components at the TA rather than just at the current project. We also want developers to be able to find reusable patterns or components easily, and we hope that the use of the Framework will make that easier through categorisation by tier and model.

- **New Function by Recombination** - We don't want to place functional limitations on the solutions that can be offered in support of business strategies, but we also don't want to specify or implement excessively flexible components. We hope to find a better balance by placing more emphasis on delivering new function by new collaborations between existing components.

- **Flexibility** - We are interested in the notion of being able to accommodate the necessary amount of change through the flexible configuration of relatively inflexible components. The analogy we use is that of bricks, which are in themselves highly inflexible, but a very flexible building material because of the variety of ways they can be combined.

- **Complexity** - While a given level of functionality probably implies some minimum level of complexity, we feel that most business systems greatly exceed such minimums. We hope to use the tiers and models to encapsulate components of all types, and to reduce the interconnections to those which have demonstrable value.

- **The Framework Applied to the Development "Business"** - The Reference Model is not limited to specific line-of-business architectures. The same concepts may be applied to other domains, such as development. There is a systems development "business" within most businesses, and it has its own strategies and goals, processes and hand-offs, application components, and technology infrastructure. The framework may help to see which of these may be shareable with the parent business.

- **Resource Utilisation** - We would like to work out how to tie the actual and expected utilisation of resources (people, facilities, and technology) into both process design and process instrumentation.

8. Experience with the Framework

8.1. Building the Processes Around the Framework

We are deploying processes to apply the framework to real projects. This will ensure that the business gets increased sharing and reduced complexity benefits from its architecture, and that the EndState architecture remains fresh and responsive to real and current needs.

A second necessary process is related to research. We would like to place high-risk elements in an explicitly experimental context, and keep them out of production projects whose definition of "success" is quite different. Research should investigate how new technologies, strategies, processes might be incorporated into the EndState architecture.

Applying the framework is reactive: it responds to specific needs of projects. Research is proactive: it tries to anticipate future project needs and do the groundwork beforehand.

8.2. Sources of components

To acquire the right set of EndState Model components, we can buy, build, or adapt.

For the Technology Tier, we can usually buy, or at least adapt. This area is relatively mature, and industry is becoming fairly consistent in their view as to what the component types should be. As CORBA [OMG 93.12.29] is exploited, we would expect to be able to buy deployable

Common Facilities, Common Services, and Object Request Broker components for this tier, as well as some Application Objects.

This architecture is more focused on the middleware, however. If we want to dig deeper into the infrastructure to determine the right set of components "under the skin" we have to look to other sources. For example, IBM Open Blueprint [IBM95] defines a number of component types that would typically lie beneath the middleware.

The Application Object Tier offers as yet few standard component definitions. If we can afford the time, we can wait for industry or vendor standards to emerge.

Or we could define our own. This approach requires both domain and architectural skill. We prefer to employ standards in order to have the option to purchase components, so if we must prepare our own component definitions, then we should make a 'best guess' as to what the standards will be, and try to be ready to converge to standard components when and if they become available. It may be useful to develop target components by classifying empirically derived information in the way that the reference model suggests:

- Use domain expertise to define a starting set of components

- Review existing systems using their descriptions to refine the definitions of the corresponding components. Analysing several implementations of the same component will enhance the final definition.

In this process, we can expect to find previously unidentified components, as well as those that are not really well formed in current implementations.

We do have some experience purchasing components for the Process and Strategy Tiers; however these have been less industry standards and more 'best-of-breed' components.

8.3 Promulgation of the Architecture Framework

The need for architectural missionary work cannot be overstated. Each area involved in each tier has to understand the relevant models: the content, use, and value. We need to learn how to communicate an architecture, and how each stakeholder sees the value.

8.4 Accumulation of Information and Understanding

The Reference Model allows us to categorise the information we are dealing with. By being able to slot a new piece of information into the appropriate tier and model, we can see more readily how it relates to other information. For example, we can see how to relate a set of operational objectives to the strengths of a particular technology.

EndState Architecture components represent a convenient "hub" around which information can be collected. And, as components become more complicated, we can further sub-divide them into sub-components to manage the complexity.

We are experimenting with various supporting technologies for the development activities which use and contribute to such information libraries. Hypertext seems promising as a way to support the multi-dimensional links called for by the Framework.

9. Conclusions

We propose a 4-tier 3-model framework for managing architectural information, and we believe that it provides us with an opportunity to address the issues stated at the outset.

The Reference Model gives us a general framework in which to articulate a EndState Model for a given line of business, facilitating a common vision based on common language and concepts.

We can then tie the EndState Architecture to an Deployable Model by mapping EM components to actual packages.

By bringing both Strategies and Processes into the scope of the Framework we have allowed clear linkage to testable statements of business issues and needs. Making technology contribute to realised business value is the key measure of IT.

Through the tiers of the models and their components, we can partition the problem space. We can better apply the right skills to the right tasks and assign responsibilities. We can handle more parallelism. We can separate issues of "what" from issues of "how" at each tier. We can further separate functional requirements from operational objectives. People are better able to see where their contribution fits, as well as those of others.

We can more clearly see where legacy systems can be recast as deployable (in fact deployed) implementations of desirable EndState components.

Future changes seem more manageable when the Framework allows us to see clearer limits to the ramifications of the proposed change, and to see which changes require new components and which require only new collaborations.

By examining our existing and future systems for useful patterns, we hope to build a repository of familiar general solutions which will help us reduce project risk and delay.

We have had some early success in attempting to use this approach to:

- store architectural information so as to help people navigate and cover the material.

- facilitate discussions with business users and IT people at various levels.

- expand project scope from IT only to include strategy and process development, and conversely to relate business initiatives to process engineering and to IT projects .

- partition discussions of requirements and solutions along the lines of skills.

- attempt to relate legacy systems to target IT and workflow components.

Obviously a great deal of research and practical effort is required to flesh out this framework and to make it the normal mode of development thought and work. We expect this framework to shape our agenda for several years, but we also expect that some important benefits will be quickly realisable.

10.   References

[BOM95]   Business Object Management Special Interest Group, Object Management Group, Inc. *OMG Business Application Architecture: White Paper,* Draft 2, October 1995

[Fox95]   Mark S. Fox, *Enterprise Integration Laboratory; Research Synopsis,* Department of Industrial Engineering, University of Toronto, July 25, 1995

[IBM95]   *Open Blueprint Technical Overview,* International Business Machine Corporation, 1995

[Jac92]   Ivar Jacobson, Magnus Christerson, Patrik Jonsson, Gunnar Overgaard, *Object-Oriented Software Engineering: A Use Case Driven Approach,* Addison-Wesley Publishing Company, 1992

[OMG 93 12.29] Object Management Group, *The Common Object Request Broker: Architecture and Specification*, Revision 1.2, 29 December 1993

[Wir90] Rebecca Wirfs-Brock, Brian Wilkerson, Lauren Wiener, *Designing Object-Oriented Software*, Prentice Hall, Englewood Cliffs, New Jersey, 1990

[Zac87] J.A. Zachman, *A framework for information systems architecture*, IBM Systems Journal Vol. 26 No. 3 1987

Abbreviations

BOMSIG Business Object Management Special Interest Group (OMG)
CORBA Common Object Request Broker Architecture
IT Information Technology
OMG Object Management Group
RM Reference Model
EM EndState Model
DM Deployable Model

Object Oriented Technology and Interoperability

An Architectural Framework for Semantic Inter-Operability in Distributed Object Systems

Rainer Kossmann

P.O. Box 3511, Station C
Ottawa, Ontario
Canada K1Y 4H7
Email: kossmann@bnr.ca Fax: (613) 763-7066

ABSTRACT. *This research paper reports results of research on semantic inter-operability in real-time, distributed object-oriented systems. It proposes an architectural framework for distributed heterogeneous object system organization. The major goals of the framework are to provide a basis of inter-operability for different kinds of object models and application domains.*

KEYWORDS: OMG, Corba, Object-Oriented, Architecture, Inter-operability.

1. Introduction

This research paper reports results of research on semantic inter-operability in real-time distributed systems[Ivannikov, 1995]. It proposes an architectural framework for distributed heterogeneous object system organization. The major goals of the proposal are to provide a basis of inter-operability for different kinds of object models and application domains.

The proposed approach is based on the following ideas:

* wide use of reflection for semantic extensions and/or transformations;
* a notion of cover - a reflection-based functional object container with possible nesting;
* three-level architectural schema that consists of views, conceptual and implementation levels.

Section 2 of the paper develops the notion of an ObjectUniverse as the set of all objects residing in a huge address space referred to as the ObjectCosmos. ObjectIdentity is represented as a CosmicAddress in this address space. Section 3 develops the notion of Cover as a hierarchically nested set of containers over the ObjectUniverse. Each cover contains a collection of objects, plus meta-objects and associated services that provide the reflective operation for objects in the cover. Section 4 develops the notion of a three schema model for the ObjectUniverse consisting of a ViewSchema, a CosmicSchema and an ImplementationSchema. Section 5 relates this work to notions of Open Repository Systems.

2. ObjectUniverse

The proposed framework is depicted in Figure 1 as a globally interconnected set of objects known as the ObjectUniverse, positioned in a huge address space referred to as the ObjectCosmos. Each object is identified by an immutable non-reusable ObjectIdentity consisting of a unique CosmicAddress within the ObjectCosmos.

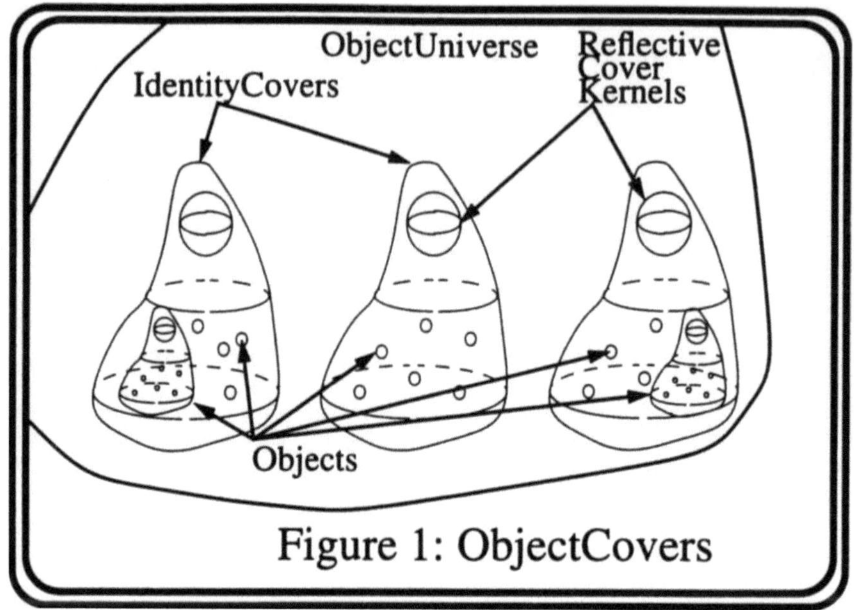

Figure 1: ObjectCovers

Objects are of two major types: as normally understood at present, and as activity causal agents referred to as sparcs. A sparc is an abstraction of the primary causal agent of any activity such as process, task, thread, co-routine, agent, etc. Sparcs are also objects having an ObjectIdentity / CosmicAddress. When a sparc invokes an operation on an object, it drives a thread through that object. Objects which have no thread operating through them are called passive objects, whereas objects which have threads being driven through them by sparcs are called active objects.

3. Covers

3.1 Introduction - Identity Cover

Objects of the ObjectUniverse are covered by semantic covers. A semantic cover can be visualized as a container for a collection of objects / meta-objects that fully and completely describes the contained objects. A key point to note is that every cover is effectively a meta-system, because it describes and controls the objects it covers. Covers are also objects.

An IdentityCover is a specific type of compositional cover that partitions the ObjectUniverse into collections of objects. In its simplest form, the IdentityCover simply lists the CosmicAddress of the objects it contains. IdentityCover are self-descriptive, i.e. they identify themselves and their content. They may contain a cover kernel which is responsible for managing the operation on objects within the IdentityCover.

Covers may be hierarchically nested as shown in Figure 1, which depicts an IdentityCover over the ObjectCosmos. The outermost cover is referred to as the ObjectUniverseCover. We utilize the notation [Cover[*]] to represent a cover in a textual description. The [*] notation is suggestive of the hierarchical nesting of covers and is capable of unambiguously identifying a specific cover instance, as in for example [Identity[BNR[Ottawa]]], which is the IdentityCover listing the identities of BNR-Ottawa objects, including the Identity of [Identity[BNR[Ottawa]]] itself.

Each IdentityCover may contain within it one or more additional orthogonal semantic covers describing further semantics properties of objects contained within the IdentityCover. In this paper we limit our examination to the additional covers [Class[*]], [Activity[*]], [Consistency[*]] and [Security[*]] described next. Other covers may also exist, for example, we note that OMG's IDL Module construct[OMG, 1992] is capable of specifying an [Interface[*]] cover over the ObjectCosmos. Another example would be a [Version[*]] cover specifying object versioning for the ObjectUniverse.

The cover kernel depicted in Figure 1 is a flexible mechanism which permits the insertion of further semantic covers into the IdentityCover. The cover kernel in an IdentityCover has an Identity-Cover-independent component, as well as an IdentityCover-dependent component which varies for each IdentityCover. The IdentityCover-independent component provides the mechanism to slot in additional covers into the IdentityCover kernel.

3.2 [Class[*]] / [Being[*]]

[Class[*]] is a semantic cover which defines the complete set of classes covering the ObjectCosmos in terms of their behaviour and attributes. Since [Class[*]] is a cover, it is of course also a meta-system.

We refer to [Identity[*]] and [Class[*]] together as [Being[*]]. [Being[*]] completely specifies the existential semantics for the ObjectUniverse. These existential semantics are in a sense analogous to the notion of real objects in the ObjectUniverse and their spatial properties: where they are, what they are made of and what can be done on or with them.

3.3 Activity[*]] / [Doing[*]]

Each sparc operative as a causal agent in the ObjectCosmos is coupled to it's own [Activity[*]] meta-object that describes the sparc's current state and sphere of influence in the ObjectCosmos. As the sparc's activity proceeds, its associated [Activity[*]] meta-object expands and contracts to encompass the objects on which it is operating. [Activity[*]] therefore completely specifies the operational semantics for the ObjectUniverse. These are in a sense analogous to causal change agents and their effects and progress in time in the real cosmos. We also refer to [Activity[*]] by the synonym [Doing[*]].

Sparcs are [Activity[*]] abstraction primitives necessary for specifying [Consistency[*]] and [Security[*]] semantics as further described below.

3.3 [Consistency[*]]

[Consistency[*]] deals with consistency semantics in the ObjectCosmos under conditions of sparcs with intersecting / colliding [Activity[*]] covers. Two [Activity[*]] meta-objects collide if they both expand to include one or more identical objects at the same time. The function of [Consistency[*]] is to ensure that the ObjectUniverse remains in a consistent state once [Activity[*]] collision ceases. The notion of transaction is an example of [Consistency[*]].

3.4 [Security[*]]

[Security[*]] semantics specify the security semantics operative in the ObjectCosmos, by specifying the 'keys' held by sparcs that permit them to open the appropriate 'locks' covering the objects they wish to access.

4. ObjectSchema

The framework deals with multiple schema analogous to the ANSI / SPARC 3-schema model for data[ANSI, 1975]. These schema are the CosmicSchema, the ImplementationSchema and the ViewSchema. These correspond approximately to the ANSI / SPARC conceptual schema, internal schema and external sub-schema.

4.1 CosmicSchema

The CosmicSchema is a description of the ObjectCosmos in terms of at least its orthogonal covers of [Being[*]], [Doing[*]], [Consistency[*]] and [Security[*]]. Figure 1 is a CosmicSchema showing only the [Identity[*]] sub-cover of [Being[*]].

4.2 ImplementationSchema

Figure 2 depicts the mapping of a CosmicSchema into an ImplementationSchema. At the ImplementationSchema, there are a number of activity engines (AE) which can be loaded with sparcs in order to perform the sparc's activity. Activity engines are generally limited to being able to perform only a few types of activity covers from the total set of activity cover types in the ObjectCosmos (e.g. UNIX SUN/OS process, active Microsoft Window, agent...).

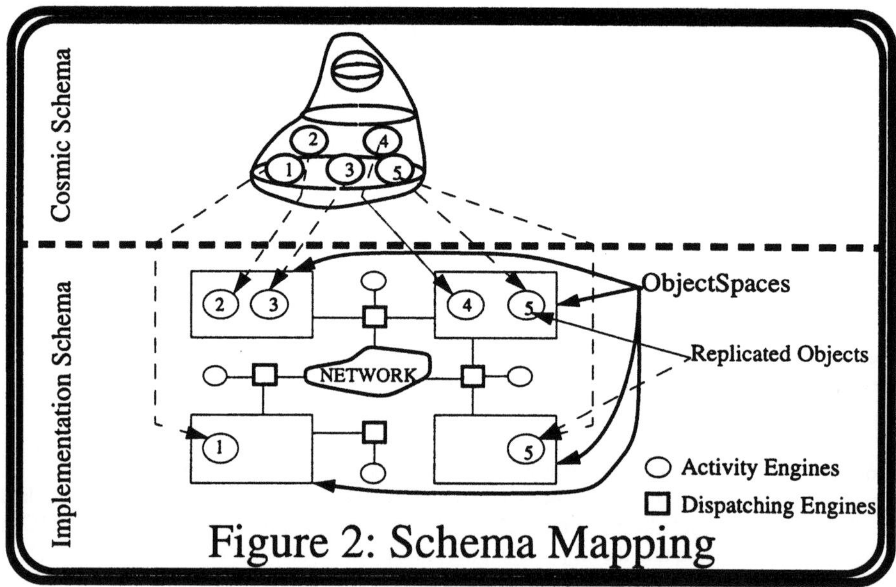

Figure 2: Schema Mapping

Objects of the ImplementationSchema are contained in memory abstractions referred to as ObjectSpaces in Figure 2. Objects have a unique ImplementationAddress within an ObjectSpace.

DispatchingEngines perform dispatch of operations on objects originating from an activity running on an ActivityEngine. DispatchEngines map the CosmicAddress of a target object into an ImplementationAddress for that object the local ObjectSpace and performs the dispatching operation. DispatchEngines therefore very similar to an OMG ORB. If the object is not local to a DispatchEngine (i.e. it is not contained in a local ObjectSpace), then the dispatch will interact with other DispatchEngines supporting the ObjectCosmos to properly dispatch the operation.

DispatchEngines have knowledge of the semantic covers over each of its ObjectSpaces and perform the appropriate semantic transformations required to support semantic inter-operability between two objects existing under their respective covers, where such semantic inter-operability is indeed possible.

Objects may also be replicated, relocated or moved within the above ImplementationSchema Platform. Such mechanisms are managed by DispatchEngines. Failures and restarts are performed by DispatchEngines or with their assistance, and generally involve relocating objects to avoid failed components ActivityEngine , DispatchEngine and ObjectSpace.

In summary, the ImplementationSchema identifies the distribution of the CosmicSchema over the ImplementationSchema Platform. I.e. it identifies the distribution of the objects of the CosmicSchema over the ActivityEngines, DispatchEngines and ObjectSpaces of the ImplementationSchema platform.

4.3 ViewSchema

A ViewSchema resides above the CosmicSchema and provides different perspectives and views of the CosmicSchema in accordance with the requirements and privileges of a viewer.

5. Enterprise Repository

The notion of hierarchically nested IdentityCovers and their distribution over ObjectSpaces is technology. At some level of [Identity[*]] below the ObjectUniverseCover of Figure 1, we apply IdentityCover technology to a specific form of human endeavour by defining the notion of EnterpriseCover. EnterpriseCovers are IdentityCovers with the additional anthropic role of being related to society and its needs[Kossmann, 1994]. We also refer to EnterpriseCover as an EnterpriseRepository. EnterpriseRepositories correspond to enterprises recognized as legal independent entities in international law such as persons, organizations and nations. The notion of a legally recognized enterprise is important because it is associated with security and authentication mechanisms that are required to be able to fully specify security semantics for the ObjectCosmos. Such mechanisms rely on SecurityCovers which map signing authorities (people) of an enterprise to sparcs (corresponding locus of action representing people) that perform activities on people's behalf. Such mappings are of course part of [Security[*]].

REFERENCES

[ANSI, 1975] "ANSI/X3/SPARC Study Group on Data Base Management Systems, 'Interim Report,'", FDT (ACM SIGMOD bulletin), Vol. 7, No. 2, 1975.

[Ivannikov et. al, 1995] "An Architectural Framework for Semantic Inter-Operability in Real-Time Distributed Object Systems", BNR Internal Report, V. Ivannikov, R. Kossmann, V. Kamensky, E. Kusikov, N. Kuzjurin, T. Kouzminov, S. Kuznetsov, B.Novikov, Y.Pogudin, L. Shabanov, I.Shevlyakov, V. Shnitman, S.Chernonozhkin, September 1995.

[Kossmann, 1994] "Repositories", ANSI X3H4 Open Repository Systems, document 94-148, R. Kossmann, July 1994.

[OMG 92.11.1, 1992] "OMG Object Management Architecture Guide (OMA Guide), Revision 2.0", Object Managment Group, September 1, 1992, OMG TC Document 92.11.1.

Semantics: the key to interoperability

Stéphane Poirier and Colin Ashford

Bell-Northern Research Ltd.,

P.O. Box 3511, Station C, Ottawa, Ontario, Canada, K1Y 4H7.

spoirier@bnr.ca | ashford@bnr.ca

ABSTRACT. *Interoperability and portability of business objects is fundamentally a question of agreed semantics—agreed syntax is of secondary importance. Agreeing common semantics is an architectural issue and involves not only high-level conceptual design but also architectural style. The process of building design offers us a model for developing interoperable and portable business objects.*

KEY WORDS: *business objects, interoperability, portability, semantics, architectural style*

1.   Introduction

In order to meet the goal of business objects supporting core business processes in a distributed, heterogeneous environment, it is crucial they exhibit true interoperability and portability. Whilst the industry has made significant progress in agreeing common protocol stacks and common APIs, this is only part of the solution. The other part of the solution is agreement on semantics in the form of common information models. We believe that there are a number of steps in the design of common information models and that two steps, conceptual design and stylistic design, deserve more attention than they have traditionally received.

1.1   Definitions

We offer the following definitions of interoperability and portability in the context of business objects:

Interoperability: the ability of two or more business objects to co-operate to achieve a common purpose.

Portability: the ability of a business object to operate correctly in different environments.

1.2   Layout of Paper

In §2 we argue that the majority of effort to meet the goal of object interoperability has been concentrated on the relatively well-understood problem of common syntactical models which has actually exacerbated the situation; in §3 we provide justifications for our contention that common information models are just as important. In §4 we propose a framework for developing common information models for telecommunications objects by means of an analogy with building architecture. In §5 we offer some conclusions.

2.   Syntactical Models

Interoperability and portability between business objects is, we believe, an architectural issue and, as such, relies on agreed models of syntax and agreed models of information.

Syntactical models in the form of standardized protocols have been developed but, rather than leading to ubiquitous interoperability, they have led to *islands* of interoperability. Where a number of protocols has evolved to address the same problem space, each has been viewed as a competing technological solution. In attempts to bridge these islands of interoperability, the industry has devised various mechanisms to automatically convert message syntaxes from one protocol to another.

Similarly, portability has been addressed by the computer industry with a number of interface models supported by different interface definition languages (IDLs), both de-facto and standardized. The current interface definition languages are unsatisfactory for two reasons:

1 they often have protocol-specific content imbedded in their syntax which leads to difficulties when trying to port objects from one environment to another; and

2 they focus on syntax—semantics are ignored—and this can lead to a breakdown in portability.

For example a stack object and a queue object have identical signatures for entering, say, integer values on to the top of the stack and on to the end of the queue respectively, namely:

<operation-name> integer

But without a statement of object semantics, the user of such an object might be surprised with the result of retrieving a previously entered value. The best that can be done with respect to object semantics with current IDLs, is to select meaningful names: in this case, possibly, "push" and "enqueue".

3.   Informational Models.

Without a common understanding of the semantics of data and the semantics of changes to data, real interoperability is unachievable. Common semantics, in the form of common information models, are the key to interoperability. Regardless of interface description languages and regardless of protocols, common semantics are required for true interoperability. Incompatible information models will prevent interoperability irrespective of the use of common carriage-protocols or common APIs. Conversely, with a common information model, interoperability can be achieved even if the protocols and APIs are different.

As an example we can cite the XJIDM management interoperability work (X/Open, 1994). The goal of the work is to permit interworking between management systems developed to conform to ISO Systems Management (ISO, 1989) standards and those developed to conform to CORBA (OMG, 1991) standards. The work entailed providing a mapping between syntactical models—GDMO (ISO, 1992) in the case of ISO Systems Management and OMG IDL (OMG, 1991) in the case of CORBA—and a mapping between the information models. The key to the success of thiswork has been that ISO Systems Management has an information model relating to systems management whereas the OMG has none. Had the OMG defined a systems management model the mapping would have been that much more difficult.

As a counter example, where the mapping was more difficult to achieve, we cite that between SNMP (Case, 1990) and ISO Systems Management where different information models of network management do, in fact, exist. The mapping turned out to be possible but had to be, nonetheless, fairly creative (NMF, 1992).

4. Building the Information Model

Building an information model is ultimately providing successive levels of semantics with, at the core, a common understanding of the system.

Some of the steps to developing an information model are well understood and require little treatment here. The initial step of identification of purpose and the final step of building the software solution, have been well explored (Rumbaugh, 1991 and Meyer, 1988). The intermediate steps of conceptual and stylistic design have been less well explored.

We devote the balance of the section to an examination of the steps required to develop and implement an information model which includes provisions for semantic description. We will illustrate the different stepsby drawing an analogy between building architectures and telecommunication architectures.

4.1 Purpose

The purpose frames the overall mission of the project by specifying requirements and constraints at a strategic level. For example:

Building: a church to meet the requirement of communal worship.

Telecommunications: a managing system to meet the requirement of remotely managing distributed systems.

In any development process the first step is requirements analysis and, as we have mentioned, this step is well understood (Jacobson, 1993 and Brook, 1975). The importance, however, of this phase of the development process to our current argument is in insuring that the rest of the information model meets these requirements.

4.2 Conceptual Design

A conceptual design is a set of technology-independent models that meets the overall mission of the project. Examples of technology-independent models might be:

Building: an arch provides support allowing the creation of open space within a building.

Telecommunications: an event-report forwards status to a managing system.

In order for a conceptual model to meet one or more strategic requirements, the semantics of such a model must be well defined.

The specification of a conceptual model should not preclude any implementation approach and can, in fact, admit to a number of equivalent implementations using different styles and technology. A

72

stylistic- and technology-independent conceptual model provides a root to which different implementations can trace their common semantics.

For example an arch provides support for the vault (the roof) of a church. Conceptually the style of the arch is irrelevant: it could be semi-circular, Gothic (pointed), or ogee but at the conceptual level it fulfills the strategic requirement—supporting the roof. Similarly an event-report carries information of an alarm condition to a managing system. At the conceptual level the style of interaction (polling versus interrupts) is irrelevant—both fulfill the strategic requirement of forwarding information to a managing system.

4.3   Architectural Style

A good architectural style provides coherence and integrity to an implementation and forms an important link between conceptual design and implementation. For example:

Building: Gothic—an architectural style which provides coherence to a vault.

Telecommunications: decentralized control (alarms are reported by event-reports) which provides coherence to an alarm-surveillance system.

Architectural style is an important stepping stone to information model refinement. It is akin to the concept of design patterns (Gamma, 1995 and Martin, 1995) with the exception that the semantics are an integral part of architectural style.

The choice of a particular building style may alter the effectiveness of a vault (width and weight ratios in the case of a Gothic arch may restrict the span of the vault). Similarly the choice of control style (alarm notification by event forwarding versus alarm notification by polling) may also alter the effectiveness of the solution. In large networks, a centralized style (alarm notification by polling) would generate a large traffic load and a decentralized style would be the preferred approach.

The degree to which interoperability can be achieved between heterogeneous implementations is also affected by the architectural style chosen for the implementations. The greater the difference between the architectural styles the greater the degree of bridging that is required. As an example, consider a bridge between a domain of implementations expecting alarm notifications by polling and a domain expecting alarm notifications by event forwarding. The bridge would be required to:

1 buffer alarm notifications emitted from the event-forwarding domain until the polling domain polls for the information; and

2 poll for alarm information from the polling domain and forward the information as alarm notifications to the event-forwarding domain.

4.4   Detailed Design

The development of the detailed design is the final step in the development process. The detailed design is the plan from which the artisan will construct the actual edifice. For example:

Building: a blueprint with the exact dimensions of the parts of the building and quantities and types of materials to be used.

Telecommunications: a computer program with interfaces specified in IDL or GDMO.

Not all construction materials fit all architectural styles; but, where they do, it is relatively straightforward to provide coherence between two implementations.

As marble and bricks can be joined using mortar to fabricate a coherent vault, so software elements in the same style can be fabricated into a coherent alarm-surveillance system. As an example in network management: it has been demonstrated that the OMG CORBA model can carry OSI Systems Management information with a straightforward mapping. Whilst the functionality of OSI Systems Management is richer than that of OMG CORBA, the basic object models are nearly identical in style (Ashford, 1993) and the management-specific models can be assembledfrom the basic CORBA models.

5. Conclusion

We have argued that:

- interoperability is intimately linked to semantics;
- common protocol and IDL syntaxes help, but are not necessary for, interoperability.
- semantics are reflected in the conceptual and stylistic design; and
- different implementations interoperate more easily if they come from identical conceptual models.

6. Abbreviations

GDMO   Guidelines for the Definition of Managed Objects.
SNMP   Simple Network Management Protocol
IDL   Interface Description Language
XJIDM   X-Open Joint Interdomain Management Group

7. References

Ashford, 1993   Ashford, C. (Ed). *Comparison of the OMG and ISO/CCITT Object Models*, Network Management Forum, Bernardsville, NJ, 1993.

Brook, 1975   Brooks, F. P., The *Mythical Man-Month*, Addison-Wesley 1975.

Case, 1990   Case, J., Fedor, M., Schofferstall, M., and Davin, J. A Simple Network Management Protocol. *Request for Comments 1157.* DDN Network Information Center, SRI International, 1990.

Gamma, 1995   Gamma, E. et al. *Design Patterns*, Addison-Wesley, 1995.

ISO, 1989   International Organization for Standardization and International Electrotechnical Commission. *Information technology — Open Systems Interconnection — Basic Reference Model — Part 4: Management Framework.* International Standard ISO/IEC 7498–4 : 1989.

ISO, 1992   International Organization for Standardization and International Electrotechnical Commission. *Information Technology — Open Systems Interconnection — Management Information Services — Structure of Management Information — Part 4: Guidelines for the Definition of Managed Objects.* International Standard ISO/IEC 10165-4 : 1992.

Jacobson, 1993   Jacobson, Ivar. *Object-oriented Software Engineering; a Use Case Driven Approach.* ACM Press, 1993.

Martin, 1995   Martin, R. Patterns: PLoP, PLoP, fizz, fizz. *Journal of Object-Oriented programming 7(8)* , 1995.

Meyer, 1988   Meyer, B. *Object-oriented Software Construction.* Prentice Hall, 1988.

NMF, 1992   The Network Management Forum. *ISO/CCITT and Internet Management Coexistence and Interworking Strategy,* TR107, Issue 1.0, 1992.

OMG, 1991   Object Management Group. *The Common Object Request Broker: Architecture and Specification*, Boulder, CO, 1991.

Rumbaugh,1991   Rumbaugh, J., et al. *Object-Oriented Modeling and Design*, Prentice Hall, 1991.

X/Open, 1994   XJIDM Taskforce. *Translation of GDMO Specifications into CORBA-IDL*, September 1994.

Business Objects Applications

Object Business Modelling, requirements and approach

Guus Ramackers and Dai Clegg [1]

Oracle Corporation
European Development Centre
Oracle Park, Guildford Road, Bittams Lane
Chertsey KT16 9RG, UK
e-mail: {gramacke, dclegg}@uk.oracle.com
fax: +44 (0)1932 873273

Abstract. *In order to exploit the advantages of object technology in large industrial Information System environments, additional enterprise orientation and user involvement are essential. Only the combination of business modelling and object-oriented design in an integrated fashion can leverage the promise of reuse and flexibility at the business level. 'Object Business Modelling' is a tool supported approach that addresses this need. Its goals are to tailor modelling to the needs of domain specialists and end-users and to hide many of the complexities of system design through application and workflow generation. The requirements to the meta-model underlying this approach are described, as well as the tool requirements for graphical manipulation of the model.*

KEY WORDS: *business modelling, requirements analysis, object-orientation, CASE tools.*

1. Introduction

Object technology holds the promise to bring reuse and flexibility to IT system development. The mechanisms to achieve this are application building by component assembly and rapid adjustment of component definitions. However, the current leverage of objects is primarily a small-town, technology oriented perspective. Reuse of low level components such as 'windows', 'widgets', 'queues' and 'sets' is possible, but these are clearly not the elements that users and enterprises expect. To make reuse work for large industrial IS environments, additional enterprise orientation and user involvement are required.

At the same time, enterprises strive to be more flexible and more aware of their business organization. In that context, business modelling forms a reflective and adaptive process in its own right (e.g. "business process re-engineering"). However, "in its own right" is the cause of considerable problems in integrating the results of business modelling with IT development, particularly workflow and application design. Given the dependency of business change on modifications of the supporting IT systems, business modelling should interface directly with system design. The object paradigm provides an excellent basis for achieving this integration.

Thus, business modelling and object-oriented design are required in an integrated fashion to achieve industrial strength business and IS improvement on a continuous basis. The combination of model based development and component assembly can leverage the promise of reuse and flexibility at the business level. Only then can IT foster business opportunities rather than a deadly embrace with the past.

It will be clear that delivering such a solution depends heavily on the availability of an object technology infrastructure. Distributed object storage and component middleware to enable

---

[1] Disclaimer: the views expressed by the authors do not necessarily coincide with those of Oracle Corporation.

object messaging in a heterogeneous computing environment are essential. However, such technology is now becoming available (OLE, COM, DSOM, OpenDoc, ...). In order to use it effectively, this technology needs to be driven from the business modelling level by generating into design and run-time environments.

In conclusion, the goal of Object Business Modelling is to bring together business process re-engineering, workflow requirements, enterprise modelling and object-oriented analysis on the basis of an integrated meta-model. Furthermore, to interface the model to an object design and implementation environment such that many complexities are hidden through default design. This must be done in such a way that reuse of integrated system descriptions (patterns and frameworks) and system flexibility are fully enabled from the business level. Finally, tool support should focus on making modelling easier for business domain experts and end-users, particularly through animated multimedia diagrams and extensive what-if experimentation.

This development effort is part of a project investigating the requirements for an enhanced form of business modelling. The current approach to business modelling supported by CASE products is usually based on an Information Engineering style of working. This approach is not expected to achieve the goals of reuse and flexibility when combined with an object-oriented design and implementation environment. The separation of function and data combined with functional decomposition makes it difficult to localize reusable components. Moreover, function models are not precise enough, in that information as to when and under which conditions a function operates is not present.

In this paper, the requirements and approach taken for Object Business Modelling and anticipated tool support are described globally, without going into detailed solutions. We assume that object-oriented application development and middleware solutions are available. In the following, model requirements are described first, followed by primary tool requirements.

2. Model Requirements

An essential requirement for a business model is that it uses terminology that is close to the way business domain experts and end-users express themselves when talking about their organization. The primary concepts in our meta-model are:

- actor
- object
- process
- event
- rule
- goal

Actors (or roles) are the responsible agents of action within an organization. They are assigned as resources to one or more business units. These represent departments, workgroups or projects. Apart from actors, objects are the other resources involved in business processes.

Objects may be either material or informational in nature. Information objects exist in two forms, namely domain objects (a.k.a. entity objects, information objects) and business objects, similar to (Casanave (*ed.*), 1995) and (Sims, 1994). Domain objects form the underlying architecture describing the information concepts essential to the business in question. However, when actors are involved in business processes, their particular view of that underlying information (which varies per actor and per process step) is modelled through business objects.

Business objects are defined as aggregates of domain objects. In addition, they define a 'filtering' or 'view' mechanism that defines precisely which attributes, relationships, operations and life cycle states are relevant for an actor in the context of a certain business process. In this two-tiered manner, information objects are integrated with the workflow model (Helfrich, 1995).

Business processes define the chains of organizational activity threading through different business units. A process is defined in terms of a sequence of process steps, each of which may again be a process at a lower level. A process step requires a set of resources (actors, objects) and has a duration, a value addition and satisfies an organizational goal. The trigger for a process to happen is the occurrence of an event.

An event may either be a state change of an object, a condition becoming true, a time event or an external event (e.g. a phone call from a customer). However, the occurrence of an event in itself may not be enough to trigger a process. The precondition rule for the step must also be satisfied. Apart from pre- and postrules, rules may be state rules or integrity rules.

It is important that the meta-model allows precise and complete specifications. This applies particularly to the availability of events and rules. These elements are required to drive reuse and flexibility since these actions require a full understanding of the conditions under which operations are performed. They become paramount if the model is not just a static description, but is also to enable model execution.

In order to support enhanced animation and simulation of business models, it is essential that the meta-model defined has an operational basis. This requires an event based model, where triggers and rules are defined as the precise conditions governing process execution. Furthermore, instances of objects and actors must form an integral part of the model. In order to aid the definition of an interpreter for business models, it is beneficial to map the meta-model to an underlying formal representation, e.g. state transition systems (Rumbaugh, 1991) or Petri nets (Ramackers, 1994).

It should be stressed, however, that business experts and system users involved in business modelling and requirements gathering should never be bothered by formal aspects. These should be fully transparent and hence relevant only to model architects and tool implementors. If a business model can only be understood in full through formalization, then it is not a good model. Thus, a three tiered model architecture is essential: a 'user specification layer' supported by tools provides graphical and textual representations of an underlying 'integrated meta-model' which in turn has a mapping to an underlying 'system formalization'. This approach guarantees that user specifications are not 'formal' in their appearance, but nevertheless sufficiently rigorous and precise.

In the same vein, programming concepts should also be eliminated. Business models do not need to be 'computationally complete', but rather present only those aspects of implemented systems which are directly driven from the business level. The model should be consistent and comprehensive for modelling organizations in its own right: concepts may only be justified as intrinsic elements of the model, rather than through outside arguments. Programming concepts, as such, have no meaning for the business domain targeted. Business experts and users will resent any business model if it gives them the impression that some form of programming is required. For this reason, we have for instance declined to use 'invariants' and rather talk about integrity rules and pre- and postrules, which can be used to express invariants, if so required.

Traditional object-oriented methods in general pay little attention to business modelling as such, e.g. (Rumbaugh, 1991). However, the methods of Martin and Odell (Martin *et al.*, 1995) and Jacobson (Jacobson *et al.*, 1994) cover at least part of this domain. We are investigating the possibility of mapping the underlying meta-models of these approaches (or at least a major part of them) to our own model. If successful, this would enable a CASE tool to display alternative notations, based on the user's method preference.

80

3. Tool Requirements

In essence, an integrated object toolset poses requirements far beyond paper-based methodologies. The true problem is one of integrating many different, partially overlapping, "views" in a flexible manner. Therefore, a set of integrated, model based development tools can only be constructed effectively on the basis of an underlying active repository. This repository provides the data integration and consistency of the meta-model supported by the tools. In addition, it must notify tools of relevant changes (caused by some other tool) through an event mechanism. Furthermore, extensibility (e.g. for supporting customized methods) requires an open repository environment.

The primary goals of an Object Business Modelling toolset must be to make modelling easier to understand for domain experts and end-users and, furthermore, to aid them in the transition to application design. As discussed, a meta-model geared towards their (communication) requirements is essential. It also requires that the model information is presented in a graphical fashion by flexible tools, with full support for using pictures, examples, prototypes and multi-media elements as part of a model.

It should be stressed, however, that graphical representations must be based on a precise and complete underlying meta-model. Otherwise, they degenerate into ambiguous drawing conventions at best. The specification model must also become more meaningful for domain experts and end-users. Hence support for example instances throughout and business model animation and simulation is a prerequisite. Finally, the tools should make experimentation with alternative models less threatening through support for what-if scenarios.

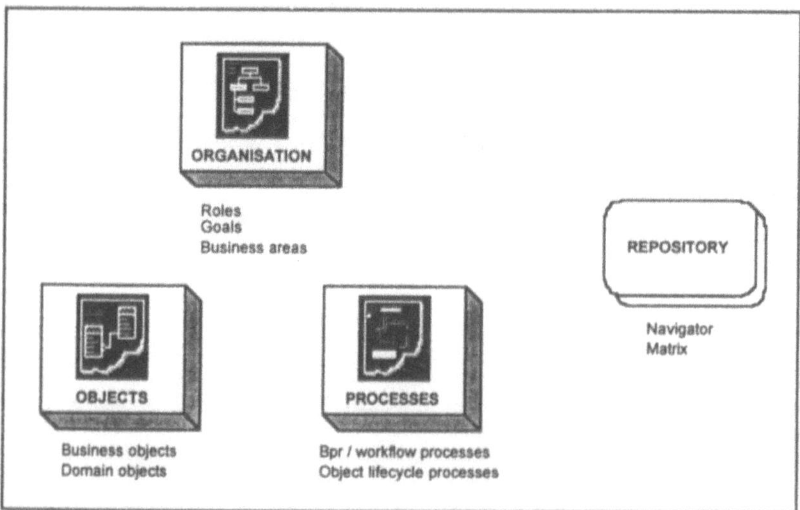

Figure 1: The user's conceptual model of the Object Business Modelling toolset.

An Object Business Modelling toolset might consist of the following modelling tools with various supported diagramming views:

- Process Modeller
  - bpr / workflow processes
  - object life cycle processes

- Object Modeller
  - business objects
  - domain objects
- Organization Modeller
  - departments and roles
  - goals
  - business areas
- Rule Editor
- Pattern Library
- Design Generator (workflow, application)

The majority of these tools are concerned with manipulating the meta-model elements discussed. Possible visualizations for the presentation of this information by the tools are illustrated below[2]. The Pattern Library and Design Generator are additional tools that offer specific functionality to enable reuse and design generation, respectively.

The Process Modeller is used to view and manipulate the business process model. This visualization is built up of horizontal "swimlanes" for each of the organization units involved in the process definition (see figure 2). This particular view allows users to focus on the communication between departments, such that interdependencies can be optimized. Each process step is executed by an actor that is part of the organization unit in question and satisfies a certain business goal. The process step requires certain objects, in a particular state, as input and produces a set of objects in an output state. Triggers and rules associated with a process step are visually annotated to it.

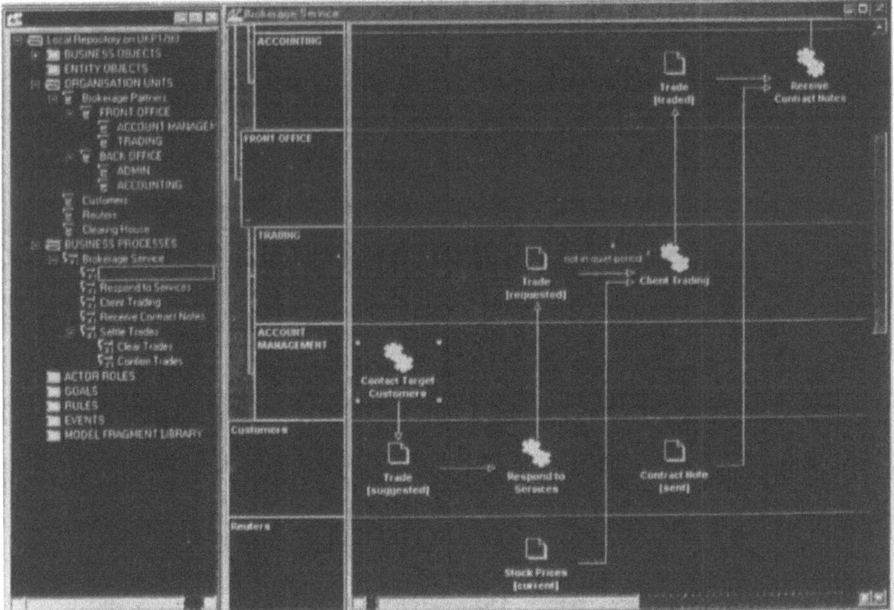

Figure 2:   A possible visualization of the process model and repository Navigator.

---

[2] The visualizations for tool manipulation illustrated in this paper are based on a prototype developed by Oracle Corporation; they may not appear in any finalized product in this form.

82

Objects may be involved in many process diagrams since these are horizontally and vertically (i.e. hierarchically) decomposed into manageable units. From an object-oriented viewpoint, however, one would like to view all state changes and events relating to a certain object type in one place. Hence, the Process Modeller also supports an "object lifecycle" view. Depending on the development process (process driven versus object driven), this view can either be derived automatically from the constructed processes, or it can be built up explicitly and used as a basis to define the various business processes it serves.

The Object Modeller represents business object definitions and domain object models in two kinds of diagrams. The domain object models provide the corporate object infrastructure for defining business objects. The latter present the user's view of a group of domain objects in the context of a certain business process (see figure 3). A business object is defined by selecting a relevant set of interrelated domain objects as its basis. Such a reusable business object definition is then tailored for each process step in which it is involved in terms of the precise subset of properties and operations it exposes. Business objects may also be composed of existing or pre-defined business object components. In this way, business objects enable reuse and flexibility because they are the prime elements that are assembled, tailored, and added to or removed from a system in support of business requirements.

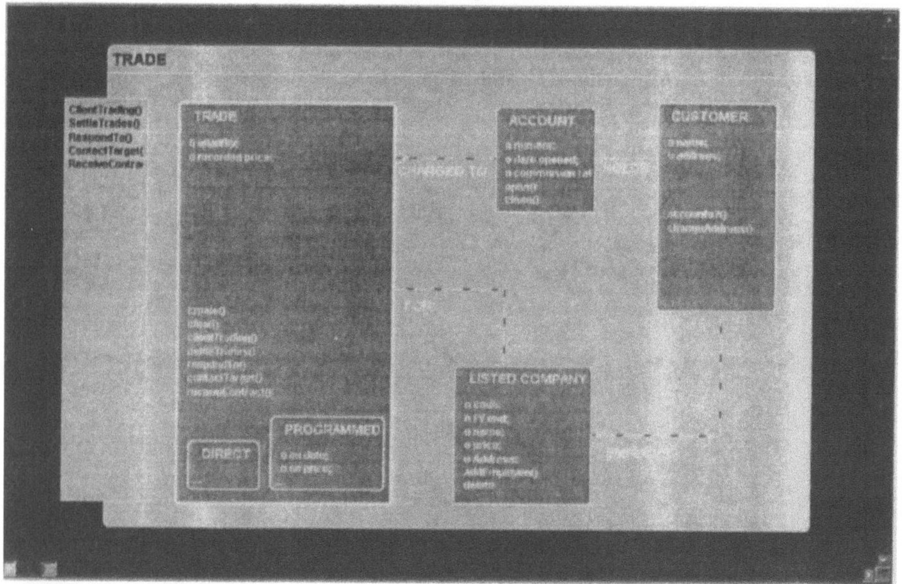

Figure 3: A possible visualization for business objects.

The Organization Modeller visualizes three different kinds of organizational hierarchies: organograms, goal hierarchies and business area architectures. Organograms (or business unit hierarchies) graphically depict the multi-level structure of organizational groups within an enterprise (see figure 4). Different types of groups such as 'organization', 'reporting group', 'department' and 'workgroup' are pre-defined and graphically distinguished (these types can be tailored by the user). Similar to the other tools, the Organization Modeller supports multiple concurrent graphical views on the repository. Hence one diagram might be used to depict "stakeholders" (external organization units at the highest level only), another for the overall picture of the organization, and separate detailed hierarchies for each reporting group. For each organization unit, a list of its roles (actors) and the people playing these roles can be defined. Both roles and persons can be assigned to multiple business units, allowing the definition of "project teams" or other cross-departmental groups.

A similar graphical visualization is used by the Organization Modeller to display goal hierarchies focusing on objectives with associated problems and critical success factors, and business area hierarchies displaying the architecture or framework of objects, processes and departments within the overall business model.

The Rule Editor is a tool to construct and manage business rules such as policies, strategies and work rules (see figure 5). It provides both a natural language description of the rule, most suited for communication with end-users, and a more structured format definition for analysts and domain experts. The construction of structured rules is supported by selecting properties of objects on an object diagram and transferring them to the Rule Editor (through "drag and drop" or "copy and paste" mechanisms). This process eliminates syntax errors and allows for storing rules in structured format, thus making them more robust for change, e.g. a name change of a referenced attribute. In addition, a list of operators (e.g. 'and', 'or', 'add') is available that can be added to rule definitions using the same mechanisms.

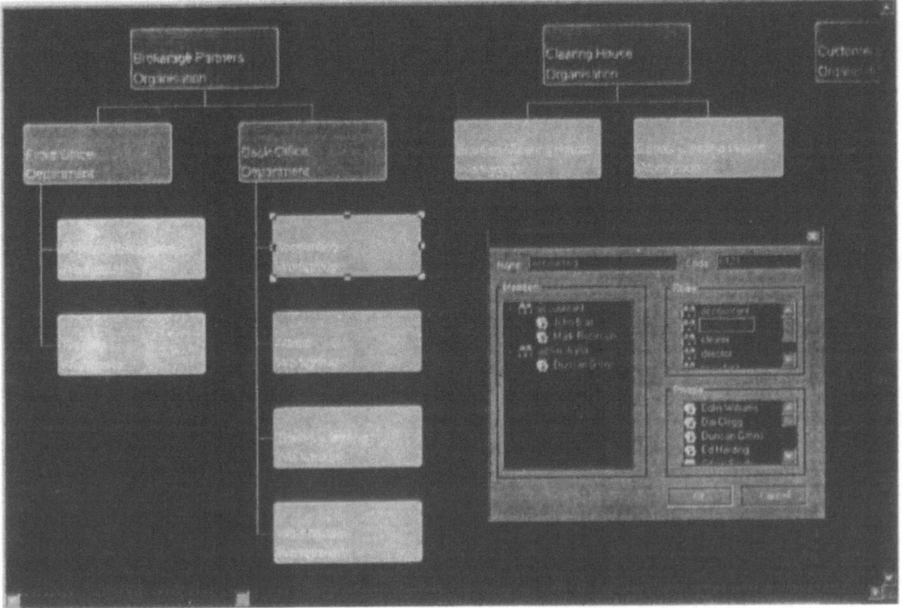

Figure 4: A possible visualization of departments and roles.

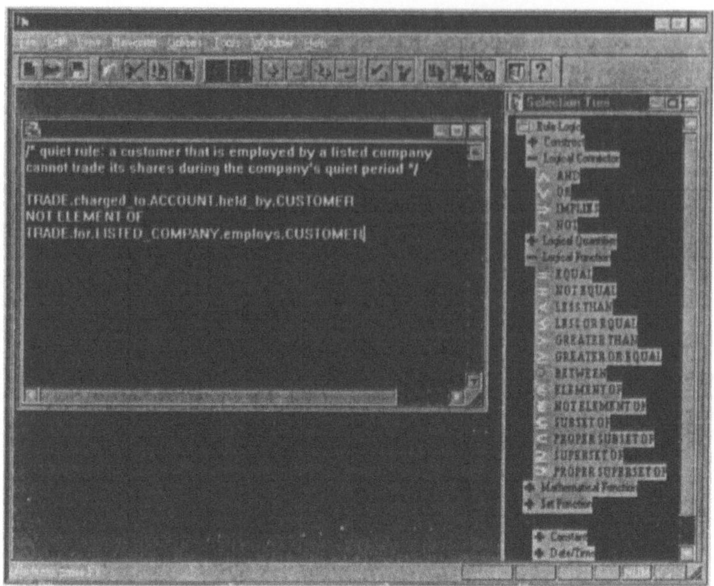

Figure 5: A possible visualization for the construction of rules.

The Pattern Library provides the mechanisms to publish model packages for reuse in a central area. Patterns (or fragments) may be domain specific, e.g. "order entry process", or they may be used generically, e.g. "resource allocation" or even "decision process with iteration". It must be easy to search for patterns in a library, inspect their contents and include them in a system (e.g. through "drag and drop"). Patterns may be included with or without specific names for model elements, i.e. the actual model, or just its structure may be reused. Furthermore, they may be included as a whole (ultimately spanning business model to implementation) or just certain aspects of their definition.

A framework can be regarded as a special pattern, i.e. one with additional conditions. Firstly, a framework is of moderate to large size, it is model complete (in the sense that all perspectives or diagrams are present) and it is a fully working solution (i.e. including implementation). A framework may be included as the basis for a (sub) system in two ways: the framework may be frozen (and modifications are made primarily through subtyping) or it may be fully modifiable.

The Design Generator functionality is aimed at hiding some of the complexities of object system design by generating a default design on the basis of a set of preferences. The structure of business concepts may differ from the classes required for efficient application design. Hence, the translation must be facilitated by automated support that produces a basic design model and the hooks for adding further detail. The process is aimed at generating (i) applications and (ii) workflow functionality across applications. The latter can be derived from the business processes defined at the modelling level. Design generation operates in three dimensions.

Firstly, the object type definitions of domain and business objects can be included as basic types that may need further refinement. They provide default database objects and application objects, respectively. In addition, many data-structure classes and user interface elements will be added to the object model at the design level.

Secondly, the behaviour of object types as defined in business processes and object lifecyles provide initial state transition diagrams for those objects at the design level. There, more detailed events and transitions will be added, without disturbing the original structure. Rules that have been specified for objects are used to generate scripting language expressions or SQL queries.

Thirdly, the business process perspective drives the workflow system design. In addition, each elementary process step can be interpreted as a "use case" that is to be detailed as an "object message diagram" to indicate how an application delivers the desired business functionality. Apart from forward design generation, a reverse engineering utility should enable a bottom up process of coupling system functionality to business requirements.

Finally, ideally, some of these tools could also be used at run-time by the end-user to define ad-hoc exceptions or modify the system on a more permanent basis by tailoring selected aspects (in a controlled and auditable manner). This applies particularly to:

- business rules
- workflow structure
- information objects (e.g. subtypes) and their views
- organization elements (business units and persons)

This would enable not only more flexibility in the development process, but also flexibility of the delivered information system (without complex re-compiling and re-installation). Again, such functionality can only be based on an integrated underlying repository, particularly one that supports both design-time and run-time environments.

4. Conclusion

Object Business Modelling addresses the need for additional user involvement and enterprise orientation that is required for mainstream adoption of object technology in corporate IS environments. Its meta-model is geared towards the communication requirements of end-users and domain specialists. The expressiveness of the model allows covering the three essential perspectives in business modelling, namely processes, objects and organization. In this way, the model enables recording business requirements, rather than technical elements.

A toolset in support of Object Business Modelling must make modelling easier for the intended target audience. This requires a clear presentation of the conceptual model to the user and support for flexible graphical views, incorporating multi media annotations, based on an underlying repository. In addition, such a toolset must hide many of the complexities of application and workflow design through preference driven generation of default designs. Conversely, it must also allow the coupling of (internally or externally) pre-developed object implementations to business object specifications.

In this way, reuse is enabled through the semantic construct of business objects (assembly and tailoring of components) together with the conditions and context for their application in business processes, and combined with the supporting mechanism of a library. Flexibility is also addressed through business objects (modifying, adding and removing components) and the process of maintaining a model based view of the current situation (thus avoiding an unmanageable collection of objects dispersed throughout the organization), combined with the supporting mechanisms of scenarios and versioning.

References

C. Casanave (*ed.*). *OMG Business Application Architecture.* Business Object Management Special Interest Group, OMG, Framingham, March 1995.

P. Helfrich. *Workflow Management Coalition: Architecture Overview and the Role of Objects.* Presentation at Business Object Management Special Interest Group, OMG, San Jose, June 1995.

I. Jacobson *et al. The Object Advantage.* Addison-Wesley, 1994.

J. Martin and J.J. Odell. *Object-Oriented Methods, a Foundation.* Prentice Hall, 1995.

G.J. Ramackers. *Integrated Object Modelling, an executable specification framework for business analysis and system design.* Thesis Publishers, Amsterdam, 1994.

J.M. Rumbaugh *et al. Object-Oriented Modelling and Design.* Prentice Hall, 1991.

O. Sims. *Business objects, Delivering cooperative objects for client-server.* McGraw-Hill, 1994.

Implementing Business Objects:
CORBA interfaces for legacy systems

Thomas Grotehen

University of Zurich
grotehen @ifi.unizh.ch

René Schwarb

SYSTOR AG
Schwarb.Rene@ch.swissbank.com

Abstract. In 1991, the OMG (Object Management Group) defined an architectural framework (OMA-Object Management Architecture) as a milestone in realizing the vision of distributed object-oriented computing. This paper describes an experiment designed to examine whether a OMA CORBA (Common Object Request Broker Architecture) implementation [OMG92, Mza95] can be successfully employed in the existing information technology environment of a bank. It provides an overview of both the benefits and the problems involved and an outlook on future technology developments in this area.

KEY WORDS:

1. Introduction

This paper provides an overview of an experiment using a CORBA implementation. The experiment [Gro94] was carried out to illustrate that CORBA implementations can be used to define a layer of business objects above existing legacy systems in a large scale financial environment. The experiment included 11 servers that allowed 12 clients to access data from legacy systems, such as product and customer data, document information, UNIX-mail, account information and data dictionary entries.

The server applications run on UNIX machines and access other UNIX, CTOS and MVS machines. The server applications can be accessed by UNIX, Windows 3.1 as well as Windows NT clients. They use IMS and DB2 transactions, a variety of interfaces to these transaction systems, Sybase Open Servers, a document generator and an interface to an electronic document management system.

This document will provide an overview of the existing legacy environment, the implemented client and server applications, and the development tools used including CORBA. In addition, we will illustrate the manner in which this evaluation confirmed our expectations with regards to the benefits derived from this architecture (integration of legacy systems, use of heterogeneous development tools and programming languages) and also show what problems can occur when using this approach.

2. The environment

2.1. Underlying legacy systems

The underlying systems represent a mixture of computing environments implemented over a period 20 years. Most data is managed by IMS database systems running on MVS. Some data is replicated on DB2 database systems also running on MVS. This data is accessed by many RTB (Real Time Banking) transactions running on IMS/DC and CICS.

A number of existing client applications run on the CTOS operating system. There are various interfaces from CTOS, DOS, OS/2 and UNIX to the transactions. In addition, interfaces exist between UNIX and CTOS, allowing access to the transactions. Furthermore, there is a DDCS (Distributed Data Communication Services) interface connecting UNIX to the MVS DB2 databases and a specific interface provides connection to an important subset (CIF-Central Information File) of the RTB transactions accessing customer and capital data.

2.2. Current development systems

Sun Solaris and the SYBASE database management system, were chosen for the server platform. The client platform was determined by banking decisions which require seamless integration of Windows applications such as MS-Word and MS-Excel with banking applications developed in-house. Therefore, client applications must run on Windows, while accessing server functionality on UNIX. The client development environment includes ART*Enterprise, Visual C++ and Enfin and the servers have been developed in C++ using several C++ development tools. The server access underlying systems run on UNIX, CTOS and MVS.

3.   CORBA business objects

One of the main problems in current projects is the use of underlying legacy systems. There are various approaches to accessing legacy data. In most cases there exists an interface function. In our experiment application developers view legacy functionality through business objects. The approach consists of three steps:

- analysis of business objects
- specification of interfaces to business objects in CORBA-IDL (Interface Definition Language)
- implementation of interfaces

The analysis of business objects is probably the most complex step. There are a variety of approaches in this area, however, most approaches do not take into consideration analysis of existing systems. We opted for the SOMA methodology [Gra94]. The result is a set of business object specifications (class cards). These have been mapped to existing transactions.
Figure 1 illustrates two simplified class cards.

Class Product	*Superclasses*	
Attributes *string* *date;*		
Public Methods **string code ();** **string condition ();** ...	*Collaborators*	
Private Methods **string date ();**	*Collaborators*	
Rules		

Class **Product Factory** *Superclasses*	
Attributes *string* *date;*	

Public Methods
**Product capture Product (in string
           code //Productcode
          in string date)
          //Datum**
	Collaborators

Private Methods	*Collaborators*
Rules	

Figure 1: Simplified class cards

The definition of interface specifications is straightforward. Each class card results in an interface. Class card public methods and attributes are mapped to attributes and operations of the interface. The following are the interface specifications derived from the class cards in Figure 1.

```
interface Product{
    string code ();
    string condition ();
    . . .
};

interface ProductClass
{
    Product captureProduct (in string code   //Productcode
                            in string date)  //Datum
};
```

Figure 2: Interfaces derived from class cards

This interface specification is used on both the client and server portion of the application. On the client side, the IDL compiler generates code (IDL stubs) which can be transparently used by client programs. (e.g. in a Visual C++ program)

The final step is to implement the server interface. In most cases we have used existing functional interfaces in a very simple architecture (one to one relationship between business objects and transactions).

4. The experiment

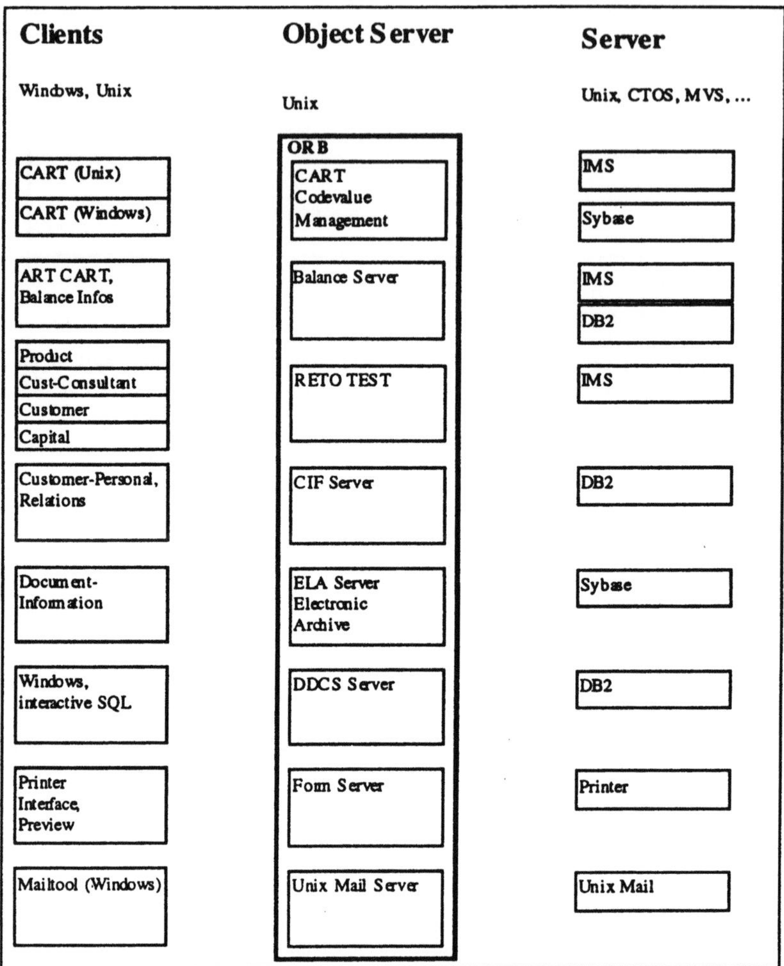

Figure 3: Clients, Object Servers and existing Systems

Most implemented applications consist of three parts. A very lean client, representing a user interface. The client runs on Windows and accesses a server via an ORB (Object Request Broker). The object server runs on Solaris and uses additional resources such as IMS transactions (minor modifications have been made in the legacy environment but they are not discussed in this paper).

Figure 3 provides an overview of the resulting system:
CART(Codes at Runtime) [KJM93] is an existing application developed in C that allows access to IMS data dictionary information at runtime. Certain CART functions access IMS databases, others

already use the Sybase database system. Our implementation provides a seamless integration of CART-services with UNIX- and Windows-C++ applications.

One of the CART UNIX client applications is the ART client. It has been developed to illustrate that client applications developed using the ART*Enterprise environment can use the functionality provided by ORB-servers. An ART-CART client simply integrates the CART functionality accessing the CART server for example to display codes. Once the integration of the CART-functionality was illustrated, a balance server providing customer balance information using two IMS-transaction was implemented.

The RETO-test application provides a small section of a retail tool. The RETO clients provide information on customers, products and customer capital. The RETO object server uses the corresponding transactions to provide data and transactions in the form of C++ classes.

The CIF (Central Information File) client provides access to CICS transactions using a Sybase network gateway and delivers data representing customer information and customer relations.

ELA (Elektronische Ablage (electronic filing)) is a product running on UNIX that allows electronic scanning, storage and access of contract documents. This access is required by several other systems. The server provides an interface to this system on UNIX that can be used by UNIX and Windows Clients in the form of C++ classes.

The DDCS server shows the implementation of an interactive Windows interface to a DB2 database using a DDCS interface. The clients allow users to specify SQL queries and convert them to DB2.

The Formula application consists of a formula server that accesses formula scripts that create documents using dynamic data from the client applications. More than 700 scripts are used to prepare customer output. The client first requests to prepare the document. The client can then retrieve a postscript file that can be viewed with a PostScript viewer or printed on the client's printer.

The Mailtool server encapsulates the UNIX mail command. We believe that this is a good example of a CORBA facility. The Windows client is a Windows Mailtool that allows Windows users to send and receive UNIX mail. The C++ classes allow Windows programmers to use the mail functionality from within their applications.

5. Benefits and problems

5.1. Benefits

In comparison with other approaches, this approach provides a variety of benefits. For example, in a two tier architecture in which legacy functionality is directly used in client applications most of the functionality concerning legacy data, such as data conversions is implemented on the client and as such is tightly coupled with the user interface. This makes it difficult to provide reusable functionality since decoupling from the user interface would be required. It also makes it difficult for other clients to reuse the functionality at runtime since code changes require recompiling and subsequent changes.

A layer of object servers makes it possible to implement new functionality separated from the user interface, and clients can use this functionality using a variety of programming languages and operating systems.

The interface to the classes is described by IDL, i.e. independent from a particular programming language. The CORBA implementation maps the IDL-descriptions to different languages supported by IDL on a variety of operating systems, making mapping reuse simple.

Furthermore, applications within different projects can use this approach to describe their interface. This results in uniform interfaces, even if the applications are developed in different programming languages. The CART application, for example, is implemented in C. Other applications developed in C++ use a set of C++ classes which are generated by the CORBA implementation to access CART.

The interface description of existing object-servers can also be used as a design documentation for a new application. Therefore, reuse is not only supported at run-time but also at the design level. In an environment where multiple applications co-exist that communicate with each other using ORB mechanisms, the development of a new application now begin with a set of uniform interface descriptions. These interface descriptions can be integrated into the design of the new application. The interface descriptions can then be used to generate the interfaces to the corresponding (existing) servers.

In summary, the main advantages of this approach are as follows:

- providing support for decoupling the user interface from the server functionality
- simple mappings of legacy functionality to object types
- uniform (standardized, object-oriented) interface descriptions
- easy reuse of applications and design specifications in a heterogeneous environment

5.2. Problems

Early CORBA adopters may face a number of problems. The technology is still in its infancy, especially as object services used by the ORB are still in a standardization and implementation phase. An example of such an object service is the transaction service. This service has already been adopted as OMG technology but not included in CORBA implementations. Therefore, applications requiring concurrent access to shared data must provide their own mechanisms for handling distributed transactions.

Services such as persistence service, concurrency service as well as recovery service are mechanisms for providing object-level transactions with ACID (Atomicity, Consistency, Isolation, Durability) properties.

Additional problems concern high availability and fault tolerance of distributed applications. These requirements have been addressed by toolkits for distributed computing such as Isis [BvR94]. Unfortunately, only a few CORBA implementations take these requirements into consideration. An example is recovery from failures in server processes. If a client has already communicated with a remote server and the server application fails, most current CORBA implementations do not provide any support to the client application. The application must be written such that it tries to recover connection to the server (which is very complicated) or the problem is left to the end user. Possible solutions to this and other problems with high availability and fault tolerance can also be achieved by combining CORBA implementations and network toolkits [OI94]. The key idea behind the Isis toolkit, for example, is that services are based on groups of processes running on different machines (more or less transparent to the user of the service).

Other problems concern network security requirements, such as the secure transmission of requests and data within a distributed system and the authentication of a request originator. If an authorized client application communicates with a server, an intruder can disconnect a client and misuse the already established connection to the server, pretending to be the client that is authorized access the server. These and other security-related problems have been addressed by mechanisms such as secure RPC (Remote Procedure Call) or Kerberos [Koh92]. Unfortunately, only a few CORBA implementations use secure messaging mechanisms. The application programmer thus has to deal with all security problems. Fortunately, most current CORBA implementations provide for convenient access to their mechanisms. Furthermore, basic security mechanisms and algorithms that fulfill a variety of security requirements exist and can easy be integrated into the applications.

6. Future developments and conclusions

In the future we must consider the following developments in the CORBA architecture:

* CORBA implementations will be integrated into operating systems
* CORBA implementations from a variety of vendors will be interoperable. (CORBA 2.0)
* Microsoft has endorsed CORBA, with the objective to integrate CORBA and OLE with COM (Common Object Model). CORBA implementations with an OLE bridge are already available
* Implementations of CORBA services will extend the functionality of CORBA implementations (COSS 1-4)
* CORBA Facilities will provide for a set of standardized services to be used by applications
* More dynamic and flexible tools (e.g. Java [SUN95]) will be available

This will lead to major changes such as changes in development tools, and the level of functionality provided. However, none of the changes require alteration to the basic concepts behind object-oriented technology. Therefore, the notion of an *interface for an object* is stable. CORBA-IDL is merely a simple description language for such interfaces. Furthermore, uniform development environments in large companies are unlikely for the near future. Heterogeneity will be the rule and a stable platform is an essential requirement for such enterprises. Therefore, building business objects based upon CORBA-IDL and using CORBA as the backbone of an enterprise architecture becomes is a reasonable approach for the integration of complex systems.

References:

[BvR94] Birman, K.,P., Van Renesse, R.(eds.): Reliable Distributed Computing with the Isis Toolkit. IEEE Computer Society Press, 1994

[Gro94] Grotehen T.: Evaluation: CORBA-Architecture, Swiss Bank Corporation, Domestic Division, Internal Report, 1994

[Gra95] Graham, I.: Migrating to Object Technology, Addison-Wesley, 1994

[KJM93] Kannappel, R., Jordan, J., Mühmel, J., Negroni, M., Oswald, U., Schwarb, R., Studer, C., Toman, J.: CART-Codes at Runtime, Requirements Planning, Final Draft, SBV Basel September 1993

[Koh92] Kohl, J.B., Neumann, C.: Kerberos V5 Specification. Internet -draft, September 1992

[Mza95] Mowbray, T.J., Zahavi, R.: The Essential CORBA, Systems Integration Using Distributed Objects, Addison-Wesley, 1995

[OI94] IONA Technologies Ltd and Isis Distributed Systems, Inc.: An Introduction to Orbix+Isis, IONA Technologies, 1994

[OMG92] Object Management Group: Common Object Request Broker Architecture. Framington, MA, 1992

[SUN95] Sun Microsystems. Java - The Language. Sun Microsystems Documentation 1995

Modeling Business Enterprises as Value-Added Process Hierarchies with Resource-Event-Agent Object Templates

Guido L. Geerts, Assistant Professor of Accounting
William E. McCarthy, Arthur Andersen Alumni Professor of Accounting

Department of Accounting, N270 North Business Complex
Michigan State University
East Lansing, MI 48824, USA

E-mail: Geerts "23358MGR@msu.edu" -- McCarthy "21277WEM@msu.edu"
Telephone: 517-355-7486   Fax: 517-432-1101

ABSTRACT: Applying object orientation to the task of modeling the value-added processes of a business enterprise is a task that should be examined both conceptually and practically. This paper does both, but its main theme is a conceptual reliance on a standardized object template -- the REA (resource-event-agent) model -- at various levels of abstraction as that template is used to model the economic activities of an enterprise. Deployment of REA concepts in business object design and implementation is a semantic strategy for increasing reusability and interoperability. We explain the components and use of REA models in the context of a simple example, and we discuss also its predictable patterns of implementation compromise. The paper finishes with a discussion of the adaptation of various object-oriented analysis and design techniques to the task of REA modeling of enterprises.

KEY WORDS: REA model, enterprise information architecture, object analysis and design patterns, accounting systems, value chain

1. Introduction

The enterprise information architecture of most businesses is composed primarily of data that concerns the input and output of various economic resources into a chain of value-adding processes or activities (Porter, 1985). For example, cash is exchanged for raw materials and labor, those materials and labor are converted into finished goods, and then the finished goods are exchanged for cash again in a cycle that (hopefully) produces more money in the end than was used at the beginning. A successful company or entrepreneur repeats this cycle many times a year or month in an effort to turn an initial outlay of cash (initial financing) into a surplus (profit) where expenditures are exceeded by revenues or where the enterprise's initial set of resources is exceeded in value by its ending set of resources.

The primary information system for tracking these chains of value-added activities in enterprises has traditionally been the firm's accounting system, an information architecture based upon bookkeeping principles originally promulgated over 500 years ago by a Franciscan monk -- Luca Pacioli -- in Venice. In its original form (which is actually the way in which most accounting instruction still takes place both in the USA and in the world), the Pacioli model of double-entry bookkeeping (Geijsbeek, 1914) forces a very narrow filter upon a very rich data environment for the specific purpose of supporting the preparation of periodic measures of net worth and net income as expressed solely in monetary terms. The development and dissemination of double-entry bookkeeping in 15th and 16th century Europe was a circumstance of both improved technology (the ability to use negative numbers and the printing press for example) and a radically different environment for economic development (the trading ventures to the East and to the Americas). Pacioli's model certainly stands as one of the stellar achievements of the Renaissance. In the succeeding five centuries, his methods have been enhanced and augmented (especially with regard to internal cost accounting), but the basic set of ideas retains both its essential structure and its preemptive call on the object categories used to type economic data in companies (Dunn and McCarthy, 1992). Proof of this preeminence is the very significant role still played by both general ledgers and accounting feeder systems based upon subsidiary ledger structures (such as accounts-receivable, accounts-payable, job-costing, and payroll) in most modern companies. As noted by a number of forward-thinking accountants (Andros *et al.*, 1992; Elliott, 1992; Fisher, 1994), the dominance of these information structures is clearly dysfunctional in modern commerce. However, their primacy in the accounting software market continues, although there are signs that information architectures with a more semantic orientation have evolved slowly and are starting to gain market share (McCarthy, 1995; Cherrington *et al.*, 1993).

It is interesting to note that although improved technology and a different economic environment were the clear catalysts for the emergence of double-entry accounting in the 15th century, these same environmental forces are often resisted vigorously by modern accountants as they struggle to preserve the technology of 15th century Venice in the modern world. With the technological shift to more semantic information architectures and object-oriented programming and with the commercial economic environment shift to "virtual enterprises" that concentrate on their own core competencies first and outsource other processes to downstream and upstream partners, the marketplace should expect to see different ways of tracking economic phenomena in the environment of the firm (i.e., new ways of "doing accounting" that make it less insular and more integrated). For the short term however, what we see primarily instead are a spate of "advanced technology" general ledgers and job-costing systems. In analogous terms, such advanced systems are a lot like ornithopters -- the attempts of more than 100 years ago at heavier-than-air flight where designers simply took an old model (how birds fly by flapping their wings) and tried to make it work with man-made technology. The breakthroughs that culminated with the Wright brothers successful flights at Kitty Hawk in 1903 started occurring when people began to attack the problems of manned flight with a clean conceptual slate, unencumbered by how the task was accomplished with only muscle power. Ironically, some of the first designs for ornithopters were constructed by Leonardo Da Vinci -- a Renaissance contemporary and collaborator of Pacioli. In a certain sense, all-encompassing general ledger systems that use multitudes of coded accounts (sometimes exceeding half a million) are the ornithopters of the 1990s -- designs whose time has passed, but whose continued "kludge" existence is partially enabled by technology and whose owners are under the illusion that conceptual re-orientation is unnecessary. Reengineers often refer to the presence of such artifacts as "paving the cow-paths."

In this paper, we have a number of purposes that relate to the design issues discussed above, especially as those design issues relate to the deployment of object-oriented technology in modern business organizations. Our first purpose is to introduce to the object-oriented implementation community a semantic framework for conceptualizing the data that tracks economic phenomena in an enterprise. This semantic framework is called the REA accounting model -- a framework for building accounting systems in a shared data environment that has been the subject of considerable conceptual and empirical research since its publication in *The Accounting Review* in 1982 (McCarthy 1982; Geerts and McCarthy 1994, 1995). As might be expected from the tone of our introductory comments, REA (Resource-Event-Agent) accounting systems do not use double-entry artifacts as essential primitive elements. Instead they use object conceptualizations (such as economic events, economic exchanges, and value chains) derived with the same abstraction methods that gave rise to the object orientation paradigm. In Section 2, we illustrate the basic ideas of REA by applying them to a sample described enterprise. Our purpose in doing this is to relieve readers of the burden of researching and reading all of the normative REA research work as it has been applied in the fields of database design, artificial intelligence, and software engineering. Having familiarized readers with our basic ideas, we use Section 3 to consider two matters: (a) the correspondences of certain REA principles with the ideas of object-oriented methodologists like Coad and Jacobson, and (b) the possibilities for building and using both individual object-oriented software design patterns and a unifying framework (Gamma *et al.*, 1995) grounded on REA templates and our own experiences with implementation heuristics. Based upon our own knowledge of the content of corporate data files and of corporate data warehouses and based additionally on empirical research like that of David (1995), we estimate that instantiations of the object patterns associated with full REA modeling could account for as much as 50-60 percent of normal corporate data stores. We finish the paper by speculating on possible research directions for work that combines semantic economic models with object orientation.

2. An REA modeling example

2.1 Sy's Fish

We begin our exposition of REA object modeling with a simple commercial example called Sy's Fish. This example is based on an actual company, but its structure has been greatly simplified for use in our explanations. The paragraphs below explain Sy's business.

> *Sy's Fish* is a family-owned distributor of seafood. From humble beginnings, Sy has expanded rapidly into multiple cities, and he provides his base of restaurant customers with over 50 types of fresh fish. Each location or store can carry all types of seafood, but they usually specialize in local favorites. Fish are purchased from local fishers, cleaned at the store, marked up outrageously, and then delivered to restaurant customers. Luckily, because of all the good-health publicity of fish and because of Sy's sterling reputation for quality and service, customers are willing to pay almost anything for fish with his name on it. All stores are very successful at present.

> Customers are allowed to buy on credit, and all pay on the last day of the month. Most employees are generalists who can perform many duties such as purchasing, cleaning, and delivering fish. Employees fill out time cards fortnightly upon which they may note the percentage of time devoted each day to buying, cleaning, and selling fish. One

employee at each store is designated as the boss, and he or she simply manages the input-processing-output of the fish. There are also a few other non-generalist employees at each store (such as cashiers).

Sy's also possesses a fleet of trucks. Painted with the firm's Poseidon logo in blue and white, the trucks are used to bring fish from the docks and to deliver fish to the restaurants. Both the truck and the employees involved in each purchase and sale of fish are noted. All trucks are leased on yearly contracts, and lease payments are made monthly. Cash receipts and disbursements are made to/from one of the multiple checking accounts of the firm.

Again, this enterprise description is abbreviated. There are other possible phenomena (such as advertising and rent expenditures or the payment of taxes) that ought to be included, but being simple with these descriptions allows us clarity in our explanations. REA methods can be scaled up to include all types of economic activity.

2.2 The basic template -- Resource-Event-Agents

A core concept in enterprise modeling of commercial activity and in microeconomics is the idea of an economic exchange -- a requited set of transactions where the enterprise gives up control over some resource (a decrement or give) in order to gain control over some other resource (an increment or take). Examples of simple exchanges might include: (1) a revenue process where inventory is decremented and cash is incremented or (2) an acquisition process where cash is decremented and supplies are incremented (we use the terms exchange, process, and activity to mean the same thing). REA modeling views all exchanges as two mirror-image economic events connected by a duality relationship that links the give and take of the exchange. The term REA comes from the object pattern of each event -- an *economic Resource* flows in or out of the enterprise in an *economic Event* that has both an inside *economic Agent* and an outside *economic Agent*.

An example of a fully instantiated REA template is shown in entity-relationship (Chen, 1976) form in Figure 1 which models the economic activity in *Sy's Fish* of leasing the trucks used to transport today's catch. The decrement event in this exchange is the monthly cash disbursement made by one of Sy's employees (a cashier) to the truck vendor; the increment event is the yearly lease contract negotiated with the vendor by a buyer.   In REA modeling, the connections between resources and events are termed **stock-flow** relationships, and the connections between events and agents are called **control** or **accountability** relationships. The connection between give events and take events is one of the central ideas of REA modeling, and it is called a **duality relationship**.

2.3 Economic event templates at different levels of abstraction

In the middle of Figure 2, an instantiated REA template is shown at a higher level of abstraction as a **process** or **activity** where the decremented resource is shown as an input and the incremented resource as an output. When all duality relationships are fully specified for an enterprise, the entrepreneurial rationale of its owner or manager (who are presumed to be *homo* *economicus*) is laid bare. No money is spent or any other resource consumed unless an identifiably more valuable resource is acquired in return. Taken as a whole, duality relationships are the glue that binds a firm's separate economic events together into rational economic processes, while stock-flow relationships weave these processes together into an **enterprise value chain** (Porter, 1985; Geerts and McCarthy, 1994) or **scenario** (Geerts, 1993). In its most general form, a value chain (as shown at the top of Figure 2) is a purposeful set of economic exchanges where an initial outlay of cash is successively converted into some types of more valuable intermediate resource and then finally converted back to cash.

Value chain processes can be decomposed into subprocesses multiple times before an enterprise modeler finds the level at which it is appropriate to explode into a full set of matched REA patterns. A working heuristic that gives an approximate start for deciding object tracking is to choose the level at which decision makers need to plan, control, and evaluate economic events and then go no lower (Hollander *et al.*, 1995). Full REA decomposition leads to a process structure of the firm shaped like a tree with only the leaf nodes fully exploded to object patterns, although it will be clear from discussions later in the paper that enforcing all duality links at the disaggregated object level cannot usually be done unless the enterprise has a very simple traceability structure. One must instead construct a process tree where many of the branch nodes have only partial patterns of REA objects specified for resource acquisition and subsequent consumption with the rest of the objects specified at lower levels.

Choosing the appropriate level at which to use the object templates is a difficult analysis process. However, REA modeling posits that it is possible to explode fully in every case at the leaf node level; it just doesn't always make cost-benefit sense to establish a measurement system to do so (see Grabski and Marsh (forthcoming) for a good example of following the patterns down to very minute levels). Predictable implementation compromises (McCarthy and Rockwell, 1989) of REA patterns will be discussed in a later section of this paper, but they are certainly one of the most promising directions for application of object-oriented technology to the task of constructing enterprise information architectures. A good example of an implementation compromise is shown at the bottom of Figure 2 where an economic event (in this case, the labor/truck consumption associated with getting fish to company locations) is decomposed to the task level (Burch, 1994, chap. 10). Tasks in REA analysis are, by definition, compromises to full specification (that is, they are economic events where an analyst doesn't try to specify full patterns). Their usefulness in building an information architecture for an enterprise is difficult to assess generally, but at the process leaf level their enumeration can be useful in integrating workflow management and activity-based-costing (ABC) analysis into those architectures.

Looking at Figure 2 from top to bottom, one can see REA information architectures at various levels of abstraction, and concomitantly, one can envision how these architectures are designed:

a. First of all, a corporate chain of value-added processes (Porter, 1985) is specified in very general terms. These high-level processes are then divided into subprocesses until the lowest level at which management needs to plan, control, and evaluate is reached.

b. Second, each process at the lowest level is exploded to illustrate in object fashion its decrement and increment events along with their flow of resources and their internal/external agents. For each process, there may often be multiple inputs/outputs leading to multiple types of increments/decrements. For example, the purchase increment in *Sy's Fish* would require two types of decrements: a labor/truck consumption event (exploded to tasks in Figure 2) and a cash disbursement event (not exploded).

c. Third, if necessitated by implementation and measurement considerations, some economic events are subdivided into tasks which are economic occurrences in time that do not have to adhere to the full pattern of REA exchanges.

d. Lastly, in an augmentation process not discussed or illustrated here, other object data types are added to the accountability infrastructure described above. Such additional objects might include those of a non-economic nature or those dealing more with hypothetical data types or opportunity costs (Geerts and McCarthy, 1994).

Ideally, the information architecture design process proceeds top down. However, the strong typing and structuring of the REA model actually allows construction to proceed at the middle or bottom levels first.

Figure 3 illustrates what an REA enterprise value chain might look like for our very simple example of *Sy's Fish*. Within each process, only the give (-) and take (+) events are shown along with their duality relationships. In narrative terms, Sy's "entrepreneurial script" proceeds as follows:

Sy uses cash from initial financing to acquire labor and trucks. His people use their own labor, his trucks, and cash to acquire and transport fish. Workers then use additional labor and the purchased stock to produce cleaned fish. Finally, Sy's employees use labor, the trucks, and the cleaned fish to acquire cash from customers, some of which is used to help repay the initial financing. At a more general level, the labor of managers (and perhaps other employees) is used to facilitate and supervise the overall set of buying, cleaning, and selling activities for each store.

The process hierarchy for Sy's Fish would have a root level process with cash in and cash out, thus representing the long-term behavior of the firm at a very abstract level. A second level would have three leaf processes (financing, payroll and truck acquisition) and one branch process (store supervision and facilitation). The buying, cleaning, and selling processes would be leaf nodes off of the store processing.

Figure 4 shows Sy's value chain in a slightly different fashion that emphasizes the driving definitional rationale for value-added processing. "Value" means value to the firm's customers, and in the final analysis, all economic exchanges or processes in a firm must be evaluated in light of their contribution to customer value. For such analysis, it is useful to think of the enterprise's final product as consisting of a portfolio of attributes, each of which customers value and are thus willing to pay for. In the case of Sy's Fish, this portfolio consists of the cleaned fish, the location of the fish (delivered via truck to the restaurant), the reputation of the fish, and the potential service that comes with the fish if needed. Reputations usually cost money (in advertising, patents, or quality control for example), as does service potential (such as being able to deliver on short notice or replace substandard catch without question). However, the rational economic entrepreneur is always willing to pay that money (the give in an upstream exchange) if it is exceeded in value-added to the customer (the take in the same exchange).

As Figure 4 illustrates in very abstract terms, an enterprise is constantly cycling through its overall value-added processing and turning cash into more cash (making a profit). In Porter's (1985) strategic terms, the company should (1) look at its overall process structure at various levels of abstraction, (2) decide where its core competencies lie by analyzing which of its processes work most efficiently (by producing output with less input) or most effectively (by producing a differentiated output), and (3) manage most carefully those processes associated with their core competencies. Companies like *Sy's Fish* gain their competitive advantage with a differentiated product and service, so he needs to pay special attention to the purchase, cleaning, and delivery of fish. Other processes can be outsourced or less carefully managed. For example, it is apparent that Sy has made such a decision with regard to his trucks, thinking that his leasing company can manage the purchase, maintenance, and management of these resources better than he can.

2.4   *Full REA modeling, interoperability of object components, and implementation compromises*

In papers that discuss the possibilities for intensional reasoning with REA-modeled economic phenomena, Geerts and McCarthy (1992a, 1995) champion the notion of **Full-REA Modeling** (or as it is called there *epistemologically adequate* enterprise schemas). In very simple terms, this notion means that there are decided benefits to an enterprise information architecture that uses the REA event pattern and its process level abstractions in a repeated top-down fashion. One of these benefits is due to the wide applicability of pattern-matching procedures on such a repeated-pattern architecture. This enables characterization of procedural business definitions (such as how to materialize and value claims) at a relatively high level of abstraction. With ad hoc enterprise information models, such procedures are simply not as applicable, and definitions tend to be single case programs.

The notion of full REA modeling has a related benefit that is especially applicable in an object-oriented environment-- it enables and enhances interoperability. At the process level of REA -- exploded to include matched give-take object patterns as portrayed in Figure 2b. -- business activities are highly congruent, both within and between firms. This means that the various acquisition cycles of a particular firm (for labor, for raw materials, for capital assets, etc.) all look like each other, and indeed, like all other cycles (revenue, conversion, logistics, etc.) in both the same company and other companies. This does not mean that all enterprises have the same information architecture; the idiosyncratic mixing and matching of economic activities in a particular company is what gives that firm its distinctive competitive advantages. Additionally, there are ample opportunities at the subprocess or task level of an REA architecture to tailor an object schema to fit a particular method of doing business. Thus, we see the opportunities to be great for enhanced interoperability in an REA environment, but we do not believe that its consistent repeated use of a single object pattern leads to monolithic implementations, a criticism sometimes heard of software packages like SAP that have similar design philosophies to REA (Semich, 1995).

One of the important lessons we have learned from years of adapting REA conceptual structures to actual implementation platforms (like files, network databases, relational databases, logic programming, and frame-structured representations) is that the patterns of implementation compromises necessitated by such adaptation become predictable (McCarthy and Rockwell, 1989). As we have mentioned previously, we believe that object-oriented technology holds great promise in this area because it will allow the programming associated with these compromises to become both reusable and transparent. Some of the most common REA implementation compromises are illustrated with *Sy's Fish* examples in Figure 5 and explained below.

a. Figure 5a shows a compromise that occurs in REA modeling when an exchange only involves parties internal to the enterprise **and** when the two halves of the exchange (give and take) are the same level of granularity. When this occurs, there is no reason to model both events independently as they are absolutely congruent. A good example of this is an issue of raw materials from stores into manufacturing (McCarthy, 1982). At the implementation level, the congruent events are folded into each other, so Sy (for example) would only track his cleaning events once.

b. Figure 5b illustrates in a variety of ways what is certainly the most prevalent type of REA compromise in common legacy-type file systems for commercial enterprises. Temporal aggregation means that objects representing occurrences in time are folded into more stable objects (usually representing people, things, or types). For example, instead of keeping a record of individual sales, common marketing or accounts-receivable packages for *Sy's Fish* might aggregate the effect of sales onto either the resource in the REA template (sales per week or month for a product), or the external agent (customer monthly sales or outstanding balance), or the internal agent (salesperson weekly sales total), or some combination of these three. Less commonly, the aggregated temporal effect of sales could be tracked on a upstream or downstream process in the value chain (aggregate sales due to a certain promotional effort or marketing campaign). Impounding the logic of temporal aggregation procedures in object design patterns (Gamma *et al.*, 1995) will be an important part of adapting object-oriented REA systems to the task of wrapping legacy systems (Winsberg, 1995).

c. Figure 5c illustrates with elements of *Sy's Fish* revenue cycle the possibilities for trading off some REA declarations (the explicit representation of an object or a relationship between objects) for procedures. For example, in many cases the relationship shown in dotted lines between the "restaurant" agent and the "cash receipt" event could be replaced at the implementation level by a procedure that circles clockwise back through the "sale" event to identify when needed the external agent for "cash receipt." In another example that actually uses elements of the temporal aggregation heuristics mentioned above, *Sy's Fish* might decide not to maintain the explicit duality link between "cash receipt" and "sale," choosing instead to aggregate the event effects over time and maintain those totals in the "restaurant" object. Such a compromise decision is a common feature (called "balance-forward") of legacy accounting systems, and again, understanding it well is a key to adapting object technology to working with those packages. Conceptual aspects of procedural-declarative tradeoffs in REA systems are discussed extensively by Geerts and McCarthy (1995).

The compromise patterns and examples illustrated above are not exhaustive. For example, Activity-Based Costing (ABC) systems are hybrid versions of REA models where procedural tradeoffs are made for many declarative links based upon similarity of event occurrence patterns (Geerts and McCarthy, 1992c). We intend in future work to encapsulate these ABC compromises and others into object design patterns (Gamma *et al.*, 1995). Readers should not also presume that all implementation compromises lead to less objects. For example, adaptation of REA to accommodate certain types of long-term claims processing (McCarthy, 1982; 1984) like stocks and bonds would lead to the basic patterns being enlarged (again in a predictable manner).

This discussion of implementation compromises concludes our survey of REA work that was conducted in the context of the *Sy's Fish* example. We move next to a discussion of how these ideas reflect similar object-oriented work by authors such as Coad, Jacobson, and Gamma *et al.*.

3. The REA model and object-oriented analysis/design methods

3.1   *REA implementation platforms -- databases, knowledge-bases, and object-oriented systems*

Until now, the REA Framework has primarily been used for design of accounting systems in a shared database environment (Cherrington *et al.*, 1993; Hollander *et al.*, 1995). Although relational database technology affords REA systems a robust implementation platform (allowing integration and flexibility in information retrieval), information technology has actually been a major constraint on taking full advantage of REA's capabilities. As described by Geerts (1993, pp. 150-2), a considerable amount of domain specific knowledge is lost during the mapping process when relational databases are used as implementation vehicles. The hierarchic and pattern-oriented descriptions of accounting phenomena are scattered over different tables and are no longer visible to the user. Additionally, procedural abstractions (such as being able to use set difference operations to calculate some claims) are lost in the details of the implementation (such as matching posted keys or identifying tuples with null values). Relational technology simply does not allow one to exploit REA's structural knowledge after implementation occurs, thereby reducing its applicability to domain-specific analysis and some heuristic design guidance.

Geerts (1993) and Geerts and McCarthy (1992a, 1995) explore the use of knowledge-based systems to overcome these restrictions. Knowledge technology enables both the explicit recording of hierarchical intensional structures and reasoning with them. Once these structures are in place, additional concepts (like the accounting definitions of claim, asset, cycle, etc.) may then be characterized in terms of REA primitives, and the implemented system will rely on these definitions to materialize conclusions. We foresee a major research opportunity here in developing a general accounting and economic phenomena framework consisting of REA-based definitions that may be shared and reused by many enterprises. However, for reasons of software reusability plus embedded support for both structuring and procedural abstraction, we believe that object-oriented tools may allow us and others to pursue this goal more readily than the knowledge-based tools (like Prolog) that we have been using thus far. Reusability is a key issue in object solutions for both analysis work as well as design work. Analysis Patterns as described by Coad (1995) clearly illustrate the reusability of analysis efforts, while Gamma *et al.* (1995) describe the reusability of design efforts. Both Coad (1995) and Jacobson *et al.* (1995) address the ideas of structuring and behavioral abstraction. In the sections below, we relate the ideas of these authors in a preliminary way to REA analysis, design, and implementation issues.

3.2 Coad patterns for analysis and behavioral abstraction

Coad (1995, p.xiv) describes patterns as something observed from something in actuality, as plans rather than specific implementations, and as templates to be followed during construction of a system. Briefly, they are blueprints providing practical and repeatable "how to" advice helpful for building object models. Clearly, important similarities as well as differences exist between Coad's patterns and the REA model as discussed in the previous section of the paper. These similarities and differences plus the implications of adapting his ideas to modeling economic phenomena with REA patterns are discussed next.

The generalized forms of the REA framework (McCarthy, 1979, 1980, 1982; Geerts and McCarthy, 1994) were derived by semantic abstraction (Chen, 1976; Smith and Smith, 1977) of actual economic transactions and by analysis of abstract accounting theories whose terms resembled the derived primitives. Additionally, REA modeling has been touted as a good blueprint for automated support of semantic database design (McCarthy and Rockwell, 1989), so it does seem that the model fits Coad's definitions for pattern use. Actually, the REA model may be considered as a constellation of integrated patterns (a kind of meta-pattern) in the Coad sense, because some of its major relationships (such as duality, stock-flow, control) are similar to Coad patterns (Transaction--Subsequent-Transaction, Transaction--Transaction-Line-Item, Participant--Transaction) for transactions which he recommends using in an integrated fashion.

Some significant differences do exist between REA models of enterprise economic phenomena and Coad transaction patterns. The REA patterns are first order models grounded in accounting and microeconomic theory, and they have well-defined design heuristics and implementation compromises associated with them. Coad's example patterns on the other hand are more generic and more wide-ranging. In the future, we expect to look at his ideas as we try to impart advice to enterprise information architects on the problem of adding non-economic objects to the REA accountability infrastructure.

As expected by object-oriented analysis, Coad describes behavioral abstractions relevant for each of his patterns. Although recognized as being important in McCarthy (1982) and as being the subject of some very general advice in Gal and McCarthy (1986), behavioral abstractions have been largely ignored for REA patterns. One of our current research efforts is to find relevant behavioral abstractions for each of the REA patterns as well as for REA-specific definitions of accounting and economic concepts. The generic patterns described by Coad are an excellent starting point for such efforts, although REA behavioral abstractions will be clearly different because of their economic specificity and their concomitant availability of domain heuristics. A good example of such adaptation is described in Geerts (1995) for the REA concept of claims. Claims are imbalances in duality relationships, and examples of behavioral abstractions (interactions) described by Coad for the highly similar but more generic *Transaction--Subsequent-Transaction* pattern are *How-Many* and *Calc-Over-Subsequent-Transactions*. Adapting and defining the relevant range for applying these behavioral abstractions involves a precise matching of different cardinality patterns corresponding to different business rules (for example, do we make just cash sales, do we allow installments, etc.).

3.3 Use Cases of Jacobson

Currently, the REA model provides domain-specific guidance in determining the information structure (static data model) of an enterprise. The behavioral emphasis posed by the object-oriented approach implies a research challenge to expand these horizons. Currently, we are looking at the integrated use of REA domain analysis and Jacobson's Use-Case analysis (Jacobson, 1992; Jacobson *et al.*, 1995). As suggested by Booch (1994, p.158), both approaches may considered as complementary. A Use Case is *a behaviorally related sequence of transactions* (Jacobson, 1992, p.127). For example, the task level diagram in Figure 2 could have be defined as four Use Cases: (1) Buy Fish Decision, (2) Actual Fish Purchase, (3) Fish Transportation, and (4) Fish Preparation. For each of the Use Cases, analysts and designers look for stereotypical patterns, for how events are related, and for how the Use Case affects objects. Each of the Use Cases is like a separate object capable of managing the variety of possible states and state transitions. In actuality for the *Sy's Fish* example, tasks such as "Load Fish" and "Drive Truck to Store" could have been considered as types of **Economic Event**, each of which would be subject to REA specifications. Instead, we decided to gather transportation information only at a higher level of abstraction. However, the Use Case provides us a stereotypical behavioral pattern that a transaction may go through. Each of the tasks may trigger a change in the "Transportation Activity" state. Jacobson et al. (1995) discuss at length how Use Cases help in reengineering. The extent to which REA value chain analysis (as discussed in Section 2) may benefit from integrated application with Use Cases needs to be explored further. However, the real challenge is to find domain-specific abstract Use Cases. Stated differently, we have to look for behavioral abstractions which hold for REA accounting and economic analysis. For example, what similarities exist between purchase orders and sales orders, what similarities exist between Use Cases dealing with different instances of duality relationships, etc.

3.4 Design patterns of Gamma, Helm, Johnson, and Vlissides

Reusability of design efforts may be accomplished at different levels of abstractions ranging from idioms to frameworks with design patterns lying somewhere in between. The design patterns of Gamma *et al.* offer solutions applicable to many different applications not just the tracking of economic phenomena, but the implementation of an REA system may rely greatly on some of these generic patterns. However, what is even more meaningful to advances in our work is the idea of building an REA system **Framework.**

Gamma et al. (1994, p.26) describe a *Framework* as "a *set of cooperating classes that make up a reusable design for a specific class of software,.*" and we believe that Frameworks may be the key solution to make REA accounting operational. As it stands today, the design of such systems relies inordinately on heuristic guidance not embedded (and hence not reusable by anyone except the human expert) in any software. The design of enterprise accounting solutions could benefit from a framework that supports the objects and interactions among objects which express the core (declarative and procedural) REA knowledge. Currently, we are building such a framework called FREACC (FRamework for REA ACCounting), and we hope to embed in it much of the analysis and design guidance (as both structural and behavioral abstractions) that was outlined in Section 2 of this paper.

4. Summary

This paper was designed first to bring the body of research associated with REA modeling to practitioners concerned with business object design and implementation. Most moderately complex suites of accounting software (i.e., client-server level) do not support reusability, interoperability, and portability very well, because they are based on a non-semantic model of enterprise business (double-entry accounting) that works well only for simple companies in manual and non-integrated environments. When business activities and organizational forms become complicated, object technology provides a platform for controlling complexity. However, for this technology to work well, its essential components must be based on object models of enterprise economic activity that have multiple levels of abstraction and integrated semantic patterns. The REA model fits these specifications very well, and we hope that readers of this work will become interested in our other empirical and normative work (available on request). A secondary purpose of the paper was to speculate on possible new directions in research that combines the ideas of REA modeling with object orientation. In the past, we have implemented and conceptualized most REA systems with database (Geerts and McCarthy, 1992b) or AI technology (McCarthy, 1987), and most commercial implementations have used traditional file structures (Cherrington *et al.*, 1993). However, this will clearly change because of the object model's embedded abilities to support structural and procedural abstractions. With the help of others, we hope to expand the model's basic components and definitions and to illustrate a wider range of its applicability.

5. References

Andros, D.P., J.O. Cherrington, and E.L. Denna. 1992. Reengineer your accounting the IBM way. *Financial Executive*. July/August. 28-31.

Booch, G. 1994. *Object-oriented analysis and design*. Benjamin Cummings, Redwood City, CA.

Burch, J. G. 1994. *Cost and management accounting: A modern approach*. West Publishing, St. Paul, MN.

Chen, P.P. 1976. The entity-relationship model - toward a unified view of data. *ACM Transactions on Database Systems*. March. 9-36.

Cherrington, J.O., W.E. McCarthy, D.P. Andros, R. Roth, and E.L. Denna. 1993. Event-driven business solutions: implementation experiences and issues. *Proceedings of the Fourteenth International Conference on Information Systems*. Orlando. 394.

Coad, P. (with D. North and M. Mayfield). 1995. *Object models: Strategies, patterns, & applications.* Prentice-Hall, Englewood Cliffs, NJ.

David, J.S. 1995. An empirical analysis of REA accounting systems, productivity, and perceptions of competitive advantage. Doctoral dissertation. Michigan State University.

Dunn, C.L. and W.E. McCarthy. 1992. Conceptual models of economic exchange phenomena: History's third wave of accounting systems. *Collected Papers of the Sixth World Congress of Accounting Historians.* Kyoto, Japan. Volume I. 133-164.

Elliott, R.K. 1992. The third wave breaks on the shores of accounting. *Accounting Horizons.* 1-21.

Fisher, J.S. 1994. What's ahead in accounting: The new finance. *Journal of Accountancy.* August. 73-76.

Gal, G. and W.E. McCarthy. 1986. Operation of a relational accounting system. *Advances in Accounting.* v.3. 83-112.

Gamma, E., R. Helm, R. Johnson, and J. Vlissides. 1995. *Design patterns: Elements of reusable object-oriented software.* Addison-Wesley, Reading, MA.

Geerts, G. 1993. Toward a new paradigm in structuring and processing accounting data. Doctoral dissertation. Free University Brussels.

Geerts, G. 1995. The semantic modeling of accounting phenomena, Working paper, Michigan State University .

Geerts, G. and W.E. McCarthy. 1992a. The extended use of intentional reasoning and epistemologically adequate representations in knowledge-based accounting systems. *Proceedings of the Twelfth International Workshop on Expert Systems and Their Applications.* Avignon, France. EC2: 321-32.

Geerts, G. and W.E. McCarthy. 1992b. Database accounting systems. *IT and accounting: The impact of information technology.* B.C. Williams and B.J. Spaul (eds.). Chapman & Hall. 159-183.

Geerts, G. and W.E. McCarthy. 1992c. The cost revolution from a data modeling point of view. Paper presented to the Congress of the European Accounting Association, Madrid, Spain. April.

Geerts. G. and W.E. McCarthy. 1994. The economic and strategic structure of REA accounting systems. Paper presented to the 300th anniversary program, Martin Luther University, Halle-Wittenberg, Germany. September.

Geerts. G. and W.E. McCarthy. 1995. Augmented intensional reasoning in knowledge-based accounting systems. Paper submitted to *Journal of Information Systems.*

Geijsbeek, J. B. 1914. *Ancient double-entry bookkeeping*. Scholars Book Co., Houston.

Grabski, S.V. and R.J. Marsh. Forthcoming. Integrating accounting and advanced manufacturing information systems: An ABC and REA approach. *Journal of Information Systems*.

Hollander, A. S., E. L. Denna, and J. O. Cherrington. 1995. *Accounting, information technology, and business solutions*. Richard D. Irwin, Chicago, IL.

Jacobson, I. 1992. *Object-oriented software engineering: A use case driven approach*. Addison-Wesley. Reading, MA.

Jacobson, I., M. Jacobson, and A. Jacobson. 1995. *The object advantage: Business process reengineering with object technology*. ACM Press. New York.

McCarthy, W.E. 1979. An entity-relationship view of accounting models. *The Accounting Review*. October. 667-86.

McCarthy, W.E. 1980. Construction and use of integrated accounting systems with entity-relationship modeling. in P. Chen, ed. *Entity-Relationship Approach to Systems Analysis and Design*. North-Holland. 625-37.

McCarthy, W.E. 1982. The REA accounting model: A generalized framework for accounting systems in a shared data environment. *The Accounting Review*. July. 554-578.

McCarthy, W.E. 1984. Materialization of account balances in the REA accounting model. Paper presented to the annual meeting of the British Accounting Association. Norwich, England. April.

McCarthy, W. E. 1987. On the future of knowledge-based accounting systems. The D.R. Scott Memorial Lecture Series. The University of Missouri. 19-42.

McCarthy, W. E. 1995. The evolution of accounting systems. Paper presented at Erasmus University, Rotterdam, The Netherlands. September.

McCarthy, W. E. and S.Rockwell. 1989. The integrated use of first-order theories, reconstructive expertise, and implementation heuristics in an accounting information system design tool. *Proceedings of the Ninth International Workshop on Expert Systems and Their Applications*. Avignon, France. EC2: 537-548.

Porter, M.E. 1985. *Competitive advantage*. The Free Press, N.Y.

Semich, J. W. 1995. C/S manufacturing: Build, buy, or reengineer? *Datamation*. September.

Smith, J.M. and D.C.P. Smith. 1977. Database abstractions: Aggregation and generalization. *ACM Transactions on Database Systems*. June. 105-133.

Winsberg, P. 1995. Legacy code: Don't bag it, wrap it. *Datamation*. May.

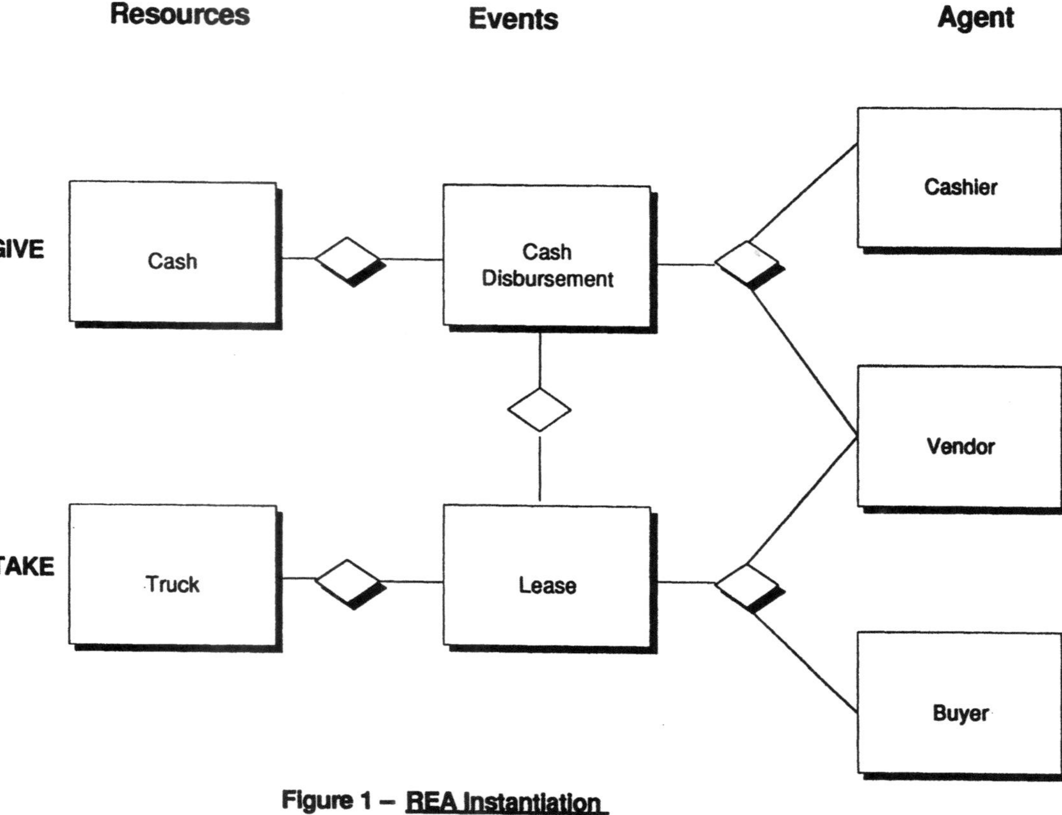

Figure 1 – <u>REA Instantiation</u>

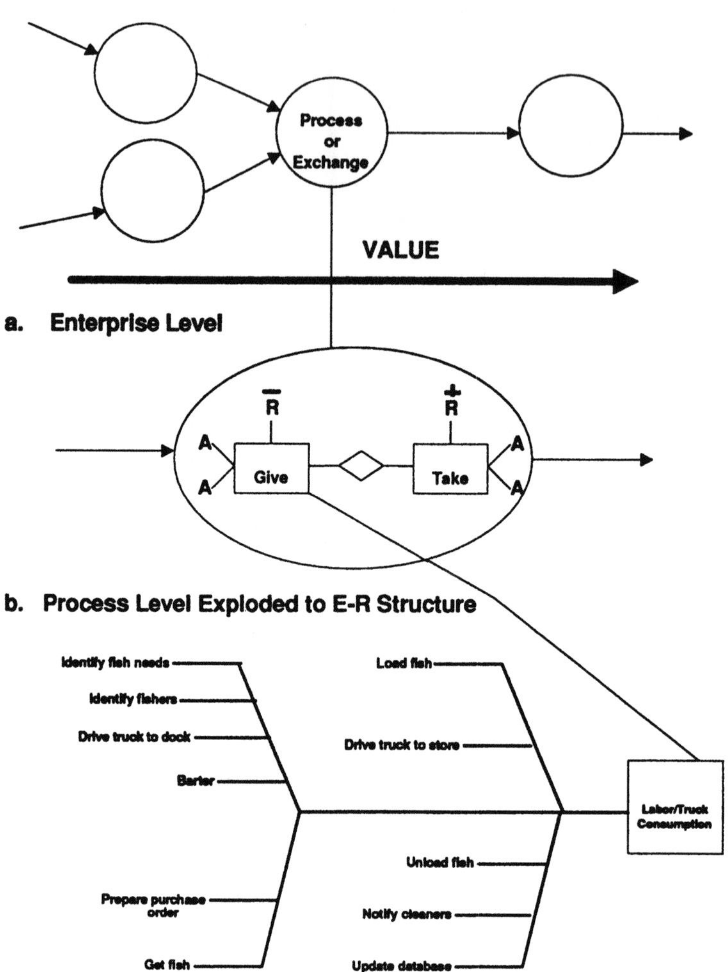

Figure 2 — **Different REA Abstraction Levels**

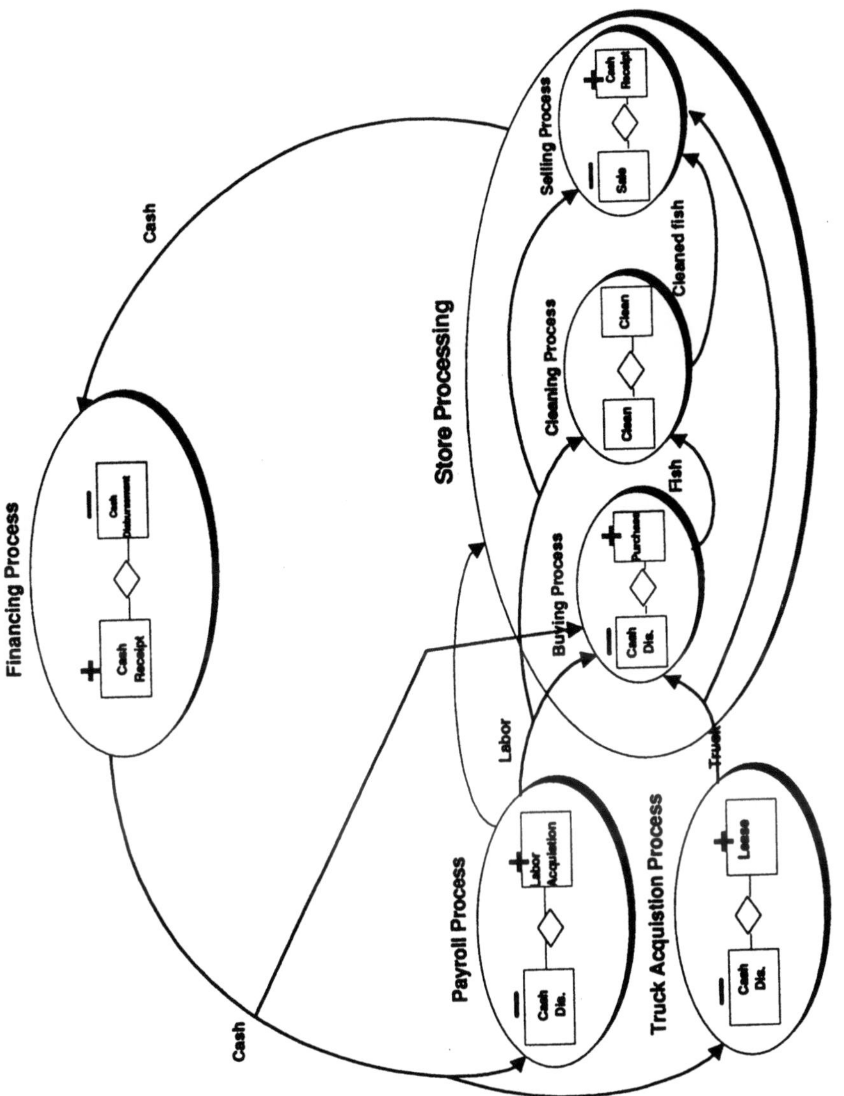

Figure 3 – "Sy's Fish" Value Chain

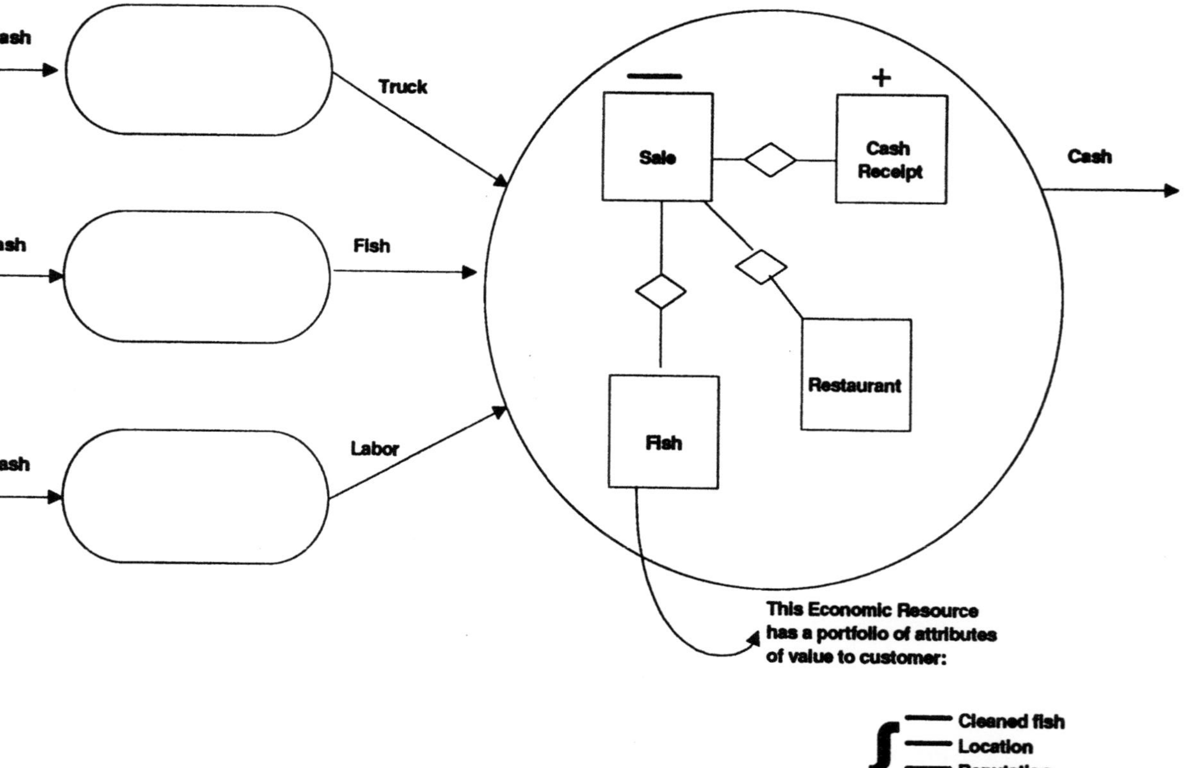

Figure 4—Customer-Driven Value Chain

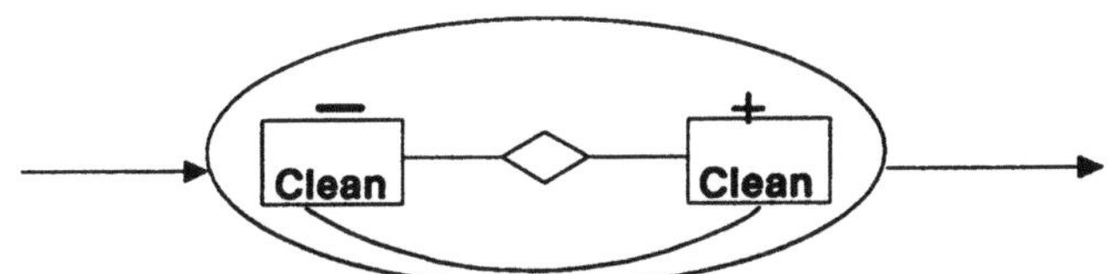

a. combine give-take (internal transfer of resource)

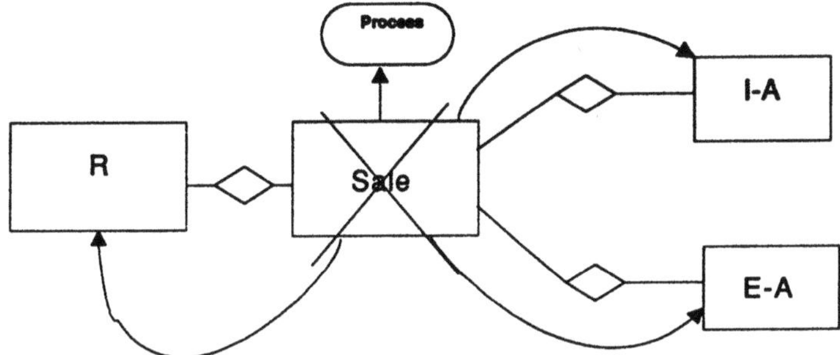

b. temporal aggregation

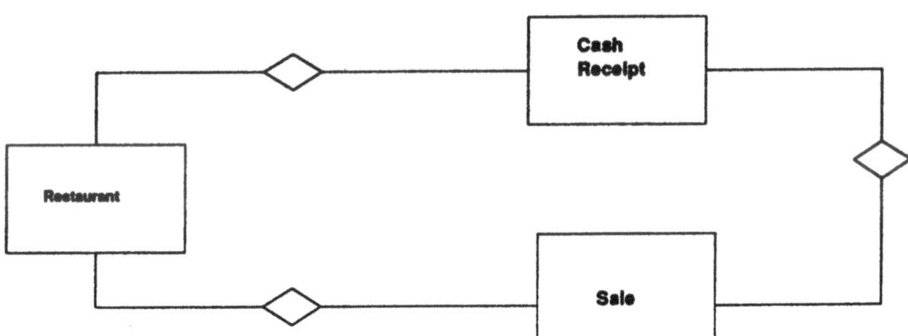

c. procedural-declarative trade-off

Figure 5 -- <u>Possible REA Compromises for Sy's Fish</u>

Managing
Object Oriented Software Development Projects

SCRUM Development Process

Ken Schwaber

Advanced Development Methods
131 Middlesex Turnpike   Burlington, MA 01803
email virman@aol.com Fax: (617) 272-0555

ABSTRACT. *The stated, accepted philosophy for systems development is that the development process is a well understood approach that can be planned, estimated, and successfully completed. This has proven incorrect in practice. SCRUM assumes that the systems development process is an unpredictable, complicated process that can only be roughly described as an overall progression. SCRUM defines the systems development process as a loose set of activities that combines known, workable tools and techniques with the best that a development team can devise to build systems. Since these activities are loose, controls to manage the process and inherent risk are used. SCRUM is an enhancement of the commonly used iterative/incremental object-oriented development cycle.*

KEY WORDS: *SCRUM SEI Capability-Maturity-Model Process Empirical*

---

1. Introduction

In this paper we introduce a development process, SCRUM, that treats major portions of systems development as a controlled black box. We relate this to complexity theory to show why this approach increases flexibility and produces a system that is responsive to both initial and additional requirements discovered during the ongoing development.

Numerous approaches to improving the systems development process have been tried. Each has been touted as providing "significant productivity improvements." All have failed to produce dramatic improvements.[1] As Grady Booch noted, "We often call this condition the software crisis, but frankly, a malady that has carried on this long must be called normal."[2]

Concepts from industrial process control are applied to the field of systems development in this paper. Industrial process control defines processes as either "theoretical" (fully defined) or "empirical" (black box). When a black box process is treated as a fully defined process, unpredictable results occur. A further treatment of this is provided in Appendix 1.

A significant number of systems development processes are not completely defined, but are treated as though they are. Unpredictability without control results. The SCRUM approach treats these systems development processes as a controlled black box.
Variants of the SCRUM approach for new product development with high performance small teams was first observed by Takeuchi and Nonaka[3] at Fuji-Xerox, Canon, Honda, NEC, Epson, Brother, 3M, Xerox, and Hewlett-Packard. A similar approach applied to software development at Borland was observed by Coplien[4] to be the highest productivity C++ development project ever

---

[1] Brooks, F.P. "No silver bullet—essence and accidents of software engineering." <u>Computer</u> 20:4:10-19, April 1987.
[2] Object Oriented Analysis and Design with Applications, p. 8, Grady Booch, The Benjamin/Cummings Publishing Company, Inc., 1994
[3] Takeuchi, Hirotaka and Nonaka, Ikujiro. January-February 1986. "The New New Product Development Game." <u>Harvard Business Review</u>.
[4] Coplien, J. "Borland Software Craftsmanship: A New Look at Process, Quality and Productivity." <u>Proceedings of the 5th Annual Borland International Conference</u>, June 5, 1994. Orlando, Florida.

documented. More recently, a refined approach to the SCRUM process has been applied by Sutherland[5] to Smalltalk development and Schwaber[6] to Delphi development.

The SCRUM approach is used at leading edge software companies with significant success. Industry analysts believe SCRUM may be appropriate for other software development organizations to realize the expected benefits from Object Oriented techniques and tools.[7]

2. Overview

Our new approach to systems development is based on both defined and black box process management. We call the approach the SCRUM methodology (see Takeuchi and Nonaka, 1986), after the SCRUM in rugby -- a tight formation of forwards who bind together in specific positions when a scrumdown is called.[8]

As will be discussed later, SCRUM is an enhancement of the iterative and incremental approach to delivering object-oriented software initially documented by Pittman[9] and later expanded upon by Booch.[10] It may use the same roles for project staff as outlined by Graham[11], for example, but it organizes and manages the team process in a new way.

SCRUM is a management, enhancement and maintenance methodology for an existing system or production prototype. It assumes existing design and code which is virtually always the case in object-oriented development due to the presence of class libraries. SCRUM will address totally new or re-engineered legacy systems development efforts at a later date.

Software product releases are planned based on the following variables :

- Customer requirements - how the current system needs enhancing.
- Time pressure - what time frame is required to gain a competitive advantage.
- Competition - what is the competition up to, and what is required to best them.
- Quality - What is the required quality, given the above variables.
- Vision - what changes are required at this stage to fulfill the system vision.
- Resource - what staff and funding are available.

These variables form the initial plan for a software enhancement project. However, these variables also change during the project. A successful development methodology must take these variables and their evolutionary nature into account.

3. Current Development Situation

Systems are developed in a highly complicated environment. The complexity is both within the development environment and the target environment. For example, when the air traffic control system development was initiated, three-tier client server systems and airline deregulation did not have to be considered. Yet, these environmental and technical changes occurred during the project and had to be taken into account within the system being built.

---

[5] Sutherland, Jeff. ScrumWeb Home Page: A Guide to the SCRUM Development Process. Jeff Sutherland's Object Technology Web Page, 1996 <http://www.tiac.net/users/jsuth/scrum/index.html>

[6] Schwaber, Ken. "Controlled Chaos: Living on the Edge." American Programmer, April 1996.

[7] Aberdeen Group. Upgrading To ISV Methodology For Enterprise Application Development. Product Viewpoint 8:17, December 7, 1995.

[8] Gartner, Lisa. The Rookie Primer. Radcliffe Rugby Football Club, 1996 <http://vail.al.arizona.edu/rugby/rad/rookie_primer.html>

[9] Pittman, Matthew. Lessons Learned in Managing Object-Oriented Development. IEEE Software, January, 1993, pp. 43-53.

[10] Booch, Grady. Object Solutions: Managing the Object-Oriented Project. Addison-Wesley, 1995.

[11] Graham, Ian. Migrating to Object Technology. Addison-Wesley, 1994.

Environmental variables include:

- Availability of skilled professionals - the newer the technology, tools, methods, and domain, the smaller the pool of skilled professionals.

- Stability of implementation technology - the newer the technology, the lower the stability and the greater the need to balance the technology with other technologies and manual procedures.

- Stability and power of tools - the newer and more powerful the development tool, the smaller the pool of skilled professionals and the more unstable the tool functionality.

- Effectiveness of methods - what modeling, testing, version control, and design methods are going to be used, and how effective, efficient, and proven are they.

- Domain expertise - are skilled professionals available in the various domains, including business and technology.

- New features - what entirely new features are going to be added, and to what degree will these fit with current functionality.

- Methodology - does the overall approach to developing systems and using the selected methods promote flexibility, or is this a rigid, detailed approach that restricts flexibility.

- Competition - what will the competition do during the project? What new functionality will be announced or released.

- Time/Funding - how much time is available initially and as the project progresses? How much development funding is available.

- Other variables - any other factors that must be responded to during the project to ensure the success of the resulting, delivered system, such as reorganizations.

The overall complexity is a function of these variables :

complexity = f(development environment variables + target environment variables)

where these variables may and do change during the course of the project.

As the complexity of the project increases, the greater the need for controls, particularly the ongoing assessment and response to risk.

Attempts to model this development process have encountered the following problems:

- Many of the development processes are uncontrolled. The inputs and outputs are either unknown or loosely defined, the transformation process lacks necessary precision, and quality control is not defined. Testing processes are an example.

- An unknown number of development processes that bridge known but uncontrolled processes are unidentified. Detailed processes to ensure that a logical model contains adequate content to lead to a successful physical model is one such process.

- Environmental input (requirements) can only be taken into consideration at the beginning of the process. Complex change management procedures are required thereafter.

120

Attempts to impose a micro, or detailed, methodology model on the development process have not worked because the development process is still not completely defined. Acting as though the development process is defined and predictable results in being unprepared for the unpredictable results.

Although the development process is incompletely defined and dynamic, numerous organizations have developed detailed development methodologies that include current development methods (structured, OO, etc.). The Waterfall methodology was one of the first such defined system development processes. A picture of the Waterfall methodology is shown in Figure 1.

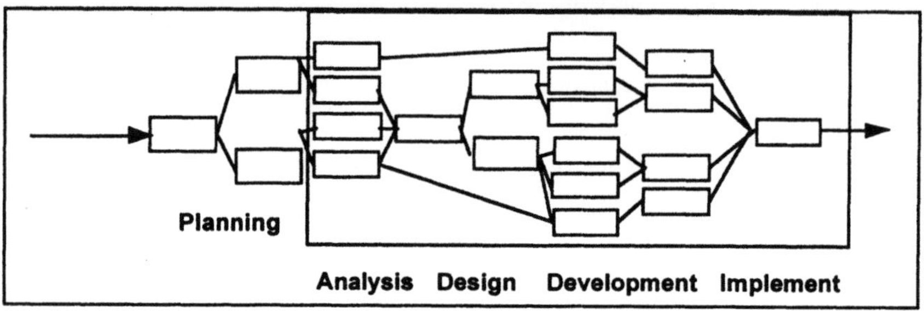

Figure 1 : Waterfall Methodology

Although the waterfall approach mandates the use of undefined processes, its linear nature has been its largest problem. The process does not define how to respond to unexpected output from any of the intermediate process.

Barry Boehm[12] introduced a Spiral methodology to address this issue. Each of the waterfall phases is ended with a risk assessment and prototyping activity. The Spiral methodology is shown in Figure 2.

The Spiral methodology "peels the onion", progressing through "layers" of the development process. A prototype lets users determine if the project is on track, should be sent back to prior phases, or should be ended. However, the phases and phase processes are still linear. Requirements work is still performed in the requirements phase, design work in the design phase, and so forth, with each of the phases consisting of linear, explicitly defined processes.

---

[12] Boehm, B.W. 1985. "A Spiral Model of Software Development and Enhancement," *from Proceedings of an International Workshop on Software Process and Software Environments*, Coto de Caza, Trabuco Canyon, California, March 27-29, 1985.

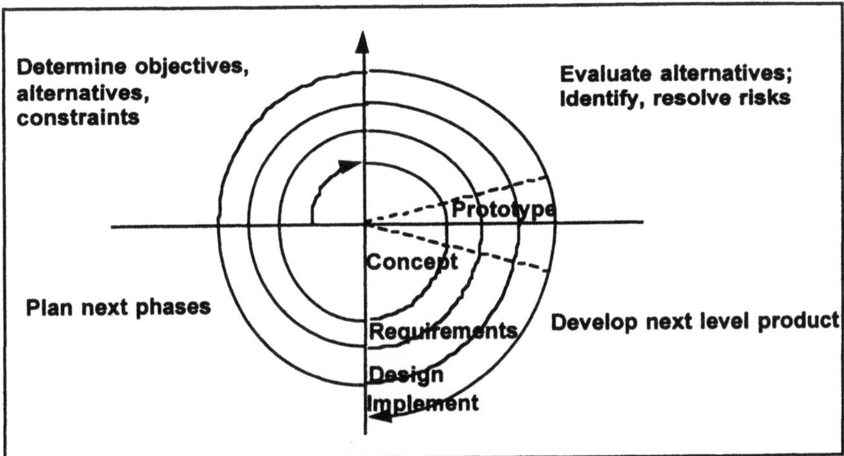

Figure 2 : Spiral Methodology

The Iterative methodology improves on the Spiral methodology. Each iteration consists of all of the standard Waterfall phases, but each iteration only addresses one set of parsed functionality. The overall project deliverable has been partitioned into prioritized subsystems, each with clean interfaces. Using this approach, one can test the feasibility of a subsystem and technology in the initial iterations. Further iterations can add resources to the project while ramping up the speed of delivery. This approach improves cost control, ensures delivery of systems (albeit subsystems), and improves overall flexibility. However, the Iterative approach still expects that the underlying development processes are defined and linear. See Figure 3.

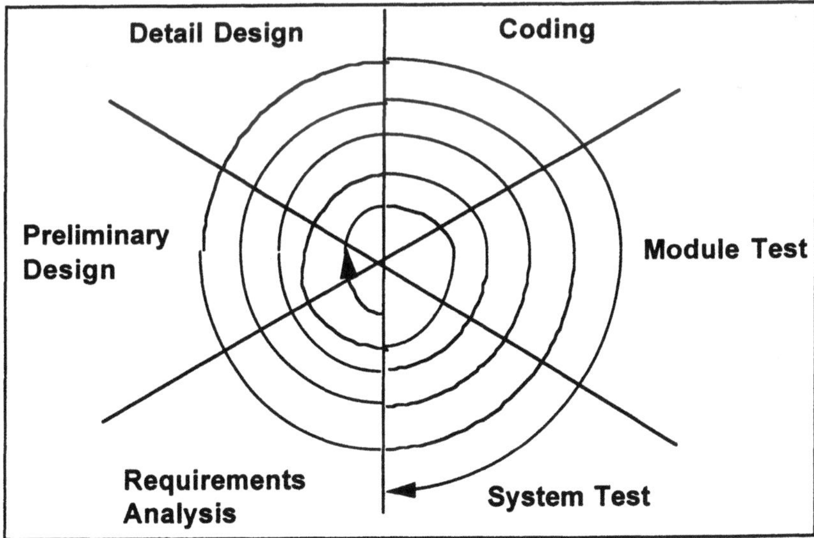

Figure 3 : Iterative Methodology

Given the complex environment and the increased reliance on new "state-of-the-art" systems, the risk endured by system development projects has increased and the search for mechanisms to handle this risk has intensified.

One can argue that current methodologies are better than nothing. Each improves on the other. The Spiral and Iterative approaches implant formal risk control mechanisms for dealing with unpredictable results. A framework for development is provided.

However, each rests on the fallacy that the development processes are defined, predictable processes. But unpredictable results occur throughout the projects. The rigor implied in the development processes stifles the flexibility needed to cope with the unpredictable results and respond to a complex environment.

Despite their widespread presence in the development community, our experience in the industry shows that people do not use the methodologies except as a macro process map, or for their detailed method descriptions.

The following graph demonstrates the current development environment, using any of the Waterfall, Spiral or Iterative processes. As the complexity of the variables increase even to a moderate level, the probability of a "successful" project quickly diminishes (a successful project is defined as a system that is useful when delivered). See Figure 4.

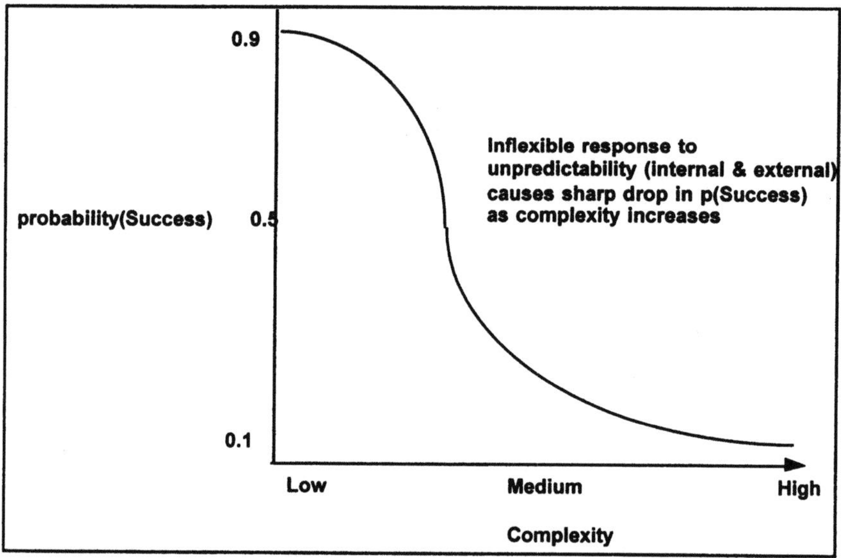

Figure 4: Defined Process Risk/Complexity Graph

4. SCRUM Methodology

The system development process is complicated and complex. Therefore maximum flexibility and appropriate control is required. Evolution favors those that operate with maximum exposure to environmental change and have optimised for flexible adaptation to change. Evolution deselects those who have insulated themselves from environmental change and have minimized chaos and complexity in their environment.

An approach is needed that enables development teams to operate adaptively within a complex environment using imprecise processes. Complex system development occurs under rapidly changing circumstances. Producing orderly systems under chaotic circumstances requires maximum flexibility. The closer the development team operates to the edge of chaos, while still maintaining order, the more competitive and useful the resulting system will be. Langton has modeled this effect in computer simulations[13] and his work has provided this as a fundamental theorem in complexity theory.

Methodology may well be the most important factor in determining the probability of success. Methodologies that encourage and support flexibility have a high degree of tolerance for changes in other variables. With these methodologies, the development process is regarded as unpredictable at the onset, and control mechanisms are put in place to manage the unpredictability.

If we graph the relationship between environmental complexity and probability of success with a flexible methodology that incorporates controls and risk management, the tolerance for change is more durable. See Figure 5.

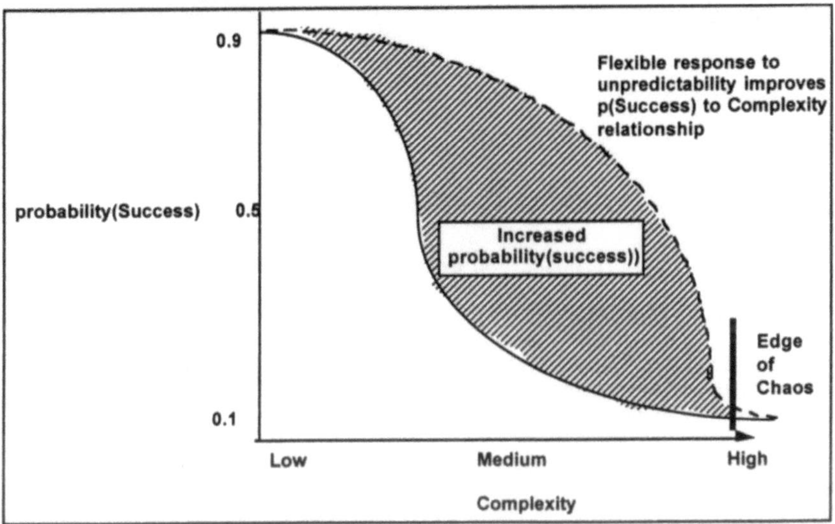

Figure 5: Risk/Complexity Comparison Graph

Figures 4 and 5 reflect software development experiences at ADM, Easel, VMARK, Borland and virtually every other developer of "packaged" software. These organizations have embraced risk and environmental complexity during development projects. Increased product impact, successful projects, and productivity gains were experienced. The best possible software is built.

Waterfall and Spiral methodologies set the context and deliverable definition at the start of a project. SCRUM and Iterative methodologies initially plan the context and broad deliverable definition, and then evolve the deliverable during the project based on the environment. SCRUM acknowledges that the underlying development processes are incompletely defined and uses control mechanisms to improve flexibility.

---

[13] Langton, Christopher. Artificial Life. In Artificial Life, Volume VI: SFI Studies in the Sciences of Complexity (Ed. C. Langton) Addison-Wesley, 1988.

The primary difference between the defined (waterfall, spiral and iterative) and empirical (SCRUM) approach is that The SCRUM approach assumes that the analysis, design, and development processes in the Sprint phase are unpredictable. A control mechanism is used to manage the unpredictability and control the risk. Flexibility, responsiveness, and reliability are the results. See Figure 6.

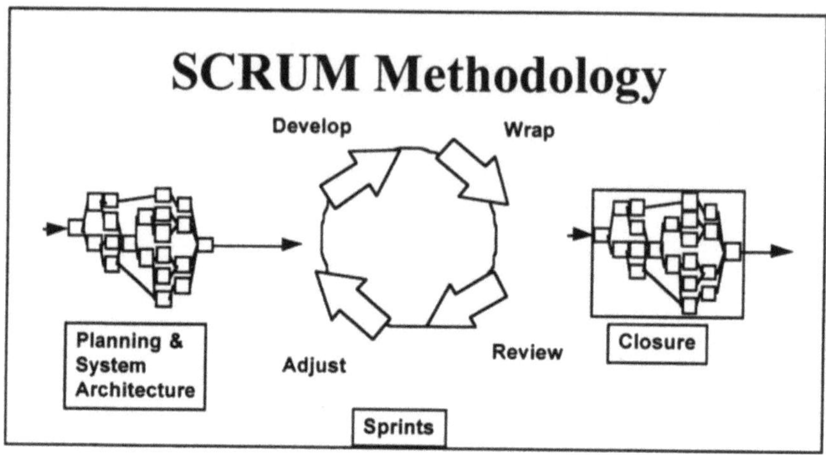

Figure 6 : SCRUM Methodology

Characteristics of SCRUM methodology are :

- The first and last phases (Planning and Closure) consist of defined processes, where all processes, inputs and outputs are well defined. The knowledge of how to do these processes is explicit. The flow is linear, with some iterations in the planning phase.

- The Sprint phase is an empirical process. Many of the processes in the sprint phase are unidentified or uncontrolled. It is treated as a black box that requires external controls. Accordingly, controls, including risk management, are put on each iteration of the Sprint phase to avoid chaos while maximizing flexibility.

- Sprints are nonlinear and flexible. Where available, explicit process knowledge is used; otherwise tacit knowledge and trial and error is used to build process knowledge. Sprints are used to evolve the final product.

- The project is open to the environment until the Closure phase. The deliverable can be changed at any time during the Planning and Sprint phases of the project. The project remains open to environmental complexity, including competitive, time, quality, and financial pressures, throughout these phases.

- The deliverable is determined during the project based on the environment.

Table 1 compares the primary SCRUM characteristics to those of other methodologies.

	Waterfall	Spiral	Iterative	SCRUM
Defined processes	Required	Required	Required	Planning & Closure only
Final product	Determined during planning	Determined during planning	Set during project	Set during project
Project cost	Determined during planning	Partially variable	Set during project	Set during project
Completion date	Determined during planning	Partially variable	Set during project	Set during project
Responsiveness to environment	Planning only	Planning primarily	At end of each iteration	**Throughout**
Team flexibility, creativity	Limited - cookbook approach	Limited - cookbook approach	Limited - cookbook approach	**Unlimited during iterations**
Knowledge transfer	Training prior to project	Training prior to project	Training prior to project	**Teamwork during project**
Probability of success	Low	Medium low	Medium	**High**

Table 1: Methodology Comparison

4.1 SCRUM Phases

Figure 7 shows the main phases and steps of the SCRUM methodology.

SCRUM has the following groups of phases:

4.1.1. Pregame
- Planning : Definition of a new release based on currently known backlog, along with an estimate of its schedule and cost. If a new system is being developed, this phase consists of both conceptualization and analysis. If an existing system is being enhanced, this phase consists of limited analysis.
- Architecture : Design how the backlog items will be implemented. This phase includes system architecture modification and high level design.

4.1.2. Game
- Development Sprints : Development of new release functionality, with constant respect to the variables of time, requirements, quality, cost, and competition. Interaction with these variables defines the end of this phase. There are multiple, iterative development sprints, or cycles, that are used to evolve the system.

4.1.3. Postgame
Closure : Preparation for release, including final documentation, pre-release staged testing, and release.

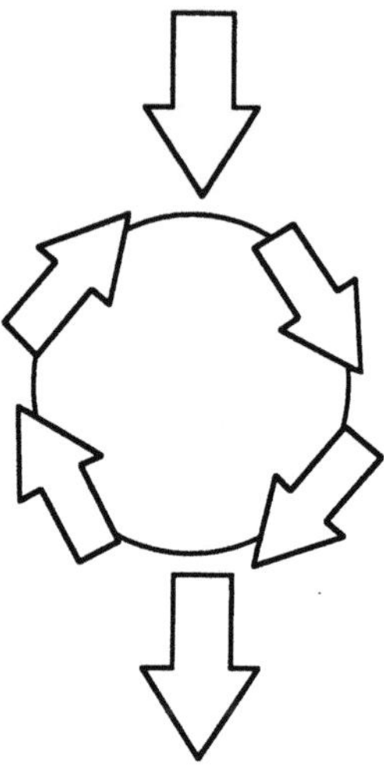

Scrum Methodology

■ **Pregame**
- **Planning**
- **System Architecture/High Level Design**

■ **Game**
- **Sprints (Concurrent Engineering)**
- **Develop (Analysis,Design,Develop)**
- **Wrap**
- **Review**
- **Adjust**

■ **Postgame**
- **Closure**

Figure 7: SCRUM Methodology

4.2 Phase Steps

Each of the phases has the following steps:

4.2.1. Planning
- Development of a comprehensive backlog list.
- Definition of the delivery date and functionality of one or more releases.
- Selection of the release most appropriate for immediate development.
- Mapping of product packets (objects) for backlog items in the selected release.
- Definition of project team(s) for the building of the new release.
- Assessment of risk and appropriate risk controls.
- Review and possible adjustment of backlog items and packets.
- Validation or reselection of development tools and infrastructure.
- Estimation of release cost, including development, collateral material, marketing, training, and rollout.
- Verification of management approval and funding.

4.2.2. Architecture/High Level Design
- Review assigned backlog items.
- Identify changes necessary to implement backlog items.
- Perform domain analysis to the extent required to build, enhance, or update the domain models to reflect the new system context and requirements.
- Refine the system architecture to support the new context and requirements.
- Identify any problems or issues in developing or implementing the changes
- Design review meeting, each team presenting approach and changes to implement each backlog item. Reassign changes as required.

4.2.3. Development (Sprint)

The Development phase is an iterative cycle of development work. The management determines that time, competition, quality, or functionality are met, iterations are completed and the closure phase occurs. This approach is also known as Concurrent Engineering. Development consists of the following macro processes :

- Meeting with teams to review release plans.
- Distribution, review and adjustment of the standards with which the product will conform.
- Iterative Sprints, until the product is deemed ready for distribution.

A Sprint is a set of development activities conducted over a pre-defined period, usually one to four weeks. The interval is based on product complexity, risk assessment, and degree of oversight desired. Sprint speed and intensity are driven by the selected duration of the Sprint. Risk is assessed continuously and adequate risk controls and responses put in place. Each Sprint consists of one or more teams performing the following:

- Develop: Defining changes needed for the implementation of backlog requirements into packets, opening the packets, performing domain analysis, designing, developing, implementing, testing, and documenting the changes. Development consists of the micro process of discovery, invention, and implementation.
- Wrap: Closing the packets, creating a executable version of changes and how they implement backlog requirements.
- Review: All teams meeting to present work and review progress, raising and resolving issues and problems, adding new backlog items. Risk is reviewed and appropriate responses defined.
- Adjust: Consolidating the information gathered from the review meeting into affected packets, including different look and feel and new properties.

Each Sprint is followed by a review, whose characteristics are :

- The whole team and product management are present and participate.
- The review can include customers, sales, marketing and others.
- Review covers functional, executable systems that encompass the objects assigned to that team and include the changes made to implement the backlog items.
- The way backlog items are implemented by changes may be changed based on the review.
- New backlog items may be introduced and assigned to teams as part of the review, changing the content and direction of deliverables.
- The time of the next review is determined based on progress and complexity. The Sprints usually have a duration of 1 to 4 weeks.

4.2.4. Closure

When the management team feels that the variables of time, competition, requirements, cost, and quality concur for a new release to occur, they declare the release "closed" and enter this phase. This phase prepares the developed product for general release. Integration, system test, user documentation, training material preparation, and marketing material preparation are among closure tasks.

4.3. SCRUM Controls

Operating at the edge of chaos (unpredictability and complexity) requires management controls to avoid falling into chaos. The SCRUM methodology embodies these general, loose controls, using OO techniques for the actual construction of deliverables.

Risk is the primary control. Risk assessment leads to changes in other controls and responses by the team.

Controls in the SCRUM methodology are :

- Backlog: Product functionality requirements that are not adequately addressed by the current product release. Bugs, defects, customer requested enhancements, competitive product functionality, competitive edge functionality, and technology upgrades are backlog items.

- Release/Enhancement: backlog items that at a point in time represent a viable release based on the variables of requirements, time, quality, and competition.

- Packets: Product components or objects that must be changed to implement a backlog item into a new release.

- Changes: Changes that must occur to a packet to implement a backlog item.

- Problems: Technical problems that occur and must be solved to implement a change.

- Risks: risks that effect the success of the project are continuously assessed and responses planned. Other controls are affected as a result of risk assessment.

- Solutions: solutions to the problems and risks, often resulting in changes.

- Issues: Overall project and project issues that are not defined in terms of packets, changes and problems.

These controls are used in the various phases of SCRUM. Management uses these controls to manage backlog. Teams use these controls to manage changes, problems. Both management and teams jointly manage issues, risks, and solutions. These controls are reviewed, modified, and reconciled at every Sprint review meeting.

4.4 SCRUM Deliverables

The delivered product is flexible. Its content is determined by environment variables, including time, competition, cost, or functionality. The deliverable determinants are market intelligence, customer contact, and the skill of developers. Frequent adjustments to deliverable content occur during the project in response to environment. The deliverable can be determined anytime during the project.

4.5 SCRUM Project Team

The team that works on the new release includes full time developers and external parties who will be affected by the new release, such as marketing, sales, and customers. In traditional release processes, these latter groups are kept away from development teams for fear of over-complicating the process and providing "unnecessary" interference. The SCRUM approach, however, welcomes and facilitates their controlled involvement at set intervals, as this increases the probability that release content and timing will be appropriate, useful, and marketable.

The following teams are formed for each new release:

<u>Management:</u> Led by the Product Manager, it defines initial content and timing of the release, then manages their evolution as the project progresses and variables change. Management deals with backlog, risk, and release content.

<u>Development teams:</u> Development teams are small, with each containing developers, documenters and quality control staff. One or more teams of between three and six people each are used. Each is assigned a set of packets (or objects), including all backlog items related to each packet. The team defines changes required to implement the backlog item in the packets, and manages all problems regarding the changes. Teams can be either functionally derived (assigned those packets that address specific sets of product functionality) or system derived (assigned unique layers of the

system). The members of each team are selected based on their knowledge and expertise regarding sets of packets, or domain expertise.

4.6 SCRUM Characteristics

The SCRUM methodology is a metaphor for the game of Rugby. Rugby evolved from English football (soccer) under the intense pressure of the game :

> Rugby student William Webb Ellis, 17, inaugurates a new game whose rules will be codified in 1839. Playing soccer for the 256-year-old college in East Warwickshire, *Ellis sees that the clock is running out with his team behind so he scoops up the ball and runs with it in defiance of the rules.*
> **The People's Chronology**, Henry Holt and Company, Inc. Copyright © 1992.

SCRUM projects have the following characteristics :

- Flexible deliverable - the content of the deliverable is dictated by the environment.

- Flexible schedule - the deliverable may be required sooner or later than initially planned.

- Small teams - each team has no more than 6 members. There may be multiple teams within a project.

- Frequent reviews - team progress is reviewed as frequently as environmental complexity and risk dictates (usually 1 to 4 week cycles). A functional executable must be prepared by each team for each review.

- Collaboration - intra and inter-collaboration is expected during the project.

- Object Oriented - each team will address a set of related objects, with clear interfaces and behavior.

The SCRUM methodology shares many characteristics with the sport of Rugby :

- The context is set by playing field (environment) and rugby rules (controls).

- The primary cycle is moving the ball forward.

- Rugby evolved from breaking soccer rules - adapting to the environment.

- The game does not end until environment dictates (business need, competition, functionality, timetable).

5. Advantages of the SCRUM Methodology

Traditional development methodologies are designed only to respond to the unpredictability of the external and development environments at the start of an enhancement cycle. Such newer approaches as the Boehm spiral methodology and its variants are still limited in their ability to respond to changing requirements once the project has started.

The SCRUM methodology, on the other hand, is designed to be quite flexible throughout. It provides control mechanisms for planning a product release and then managing variables as the project progresses. This enables organizations to change the project and deliverables at any point in time, delivering the most appropriate release.

The SCRUM methodology frees developers to devise the most ingenious solutions throughout the project, as learning occurs and the environment changes.

Small, collaborative teams of developers are able to share tacit knowledge about development processes. An excellent training environment for all parties is provided.

Object Oriented technology provides the basis for the SCRUM methodology. Objects, or product features, offer a discrete and manageable environment. Procedural code, with its many and intertwined interfaces, is inappropriate for the SCRUM methodology. SCRUM may be selectively applied to procedural systems with clean interfaces and strong data orientation.

6. SCRUM Project Estimating

SCRUM projects can be estimated using standard function point estimating. However, it is advisable to estimate productivity at approximately twice the current metric. The estimate is only for starting purposes, however, since the overall timetable and cost are determined dynamically in response to the environmental factors.
Our observations have led us to conclude that SCRUM projects have both velocity and acceleration. In terms of functions delivered, or backlog items completed :

- initial velocity and acceleration are low as infrastructure is built/modified
- as base functionality is put into objects, acceleration increases
- acceleration decreases and velocity remains sustainably high

Further development in metrics for empirical processes is required.

<u>References</u>

1. Aberdeen Group. <u>Upgrading To ISV Methodology For Enterprise Application Development</u>. Product Viewpoint 8:17, December 7, 1995.

2. Bach, James. "Process Evolution in a Mad World." Borland International, Scotts Valley, CA.

3. Bach, James. "The Challenge of "Good Enough" Software", American Programmer, October 1995.

4. Boehm, B.W. 1985. "A Spiral Model of Software Development and Enhancement," *from Proceedings of an International Workshop on Software Process and Software Environments,* Coto de Caza, Trabuco Canyon, California, March 27-29, 1985.

5. Booch, Grady. <u>Object Oriented Analysis and Design with Applications</u>. The Benjamin/Cummings Publishing Company, Inc., 1994, p. 8

6. Booch, Grady. <u>Object Solutions: Managing the Object-Oriented Project</u>. Addison-Wesley, 1995.

7. Brooks, F.P. "No silver bullet—essence and accidents of software engineering." <u>Computer</u> 20:4:10-19, April 1987.

8. Coplien, J. "Borland Software Craftsmanship: A New Look at Process, Quality and Productivity." Proceedings of the 5th Annual Borland International Conference, June 5, 1994. Orlando, Florida.

9. DeGrace, P. and Hulet Stahl, L. 1990. *Wicked Problems, Righteous Solutions*. Yourdon Press

10. Gartner, Lisa. The Rookie Primer. Radcliffe Rugby Football Club, 1996 <http://vail.al.arizona.edu/rugby/rad/rookie_primer.html>

11. Gleick, J. 1987. *Chaos, Making A New Science*. Penguin Books.

12. Graham, Ian. Migrating to Object Technology. Addison-Wesley, 1994.

13. Kahn, D. and Sutherland, J. March-April 1994. "Object Insider: Let's start under-promising and over-delivering on OT." Object Magazine.

14. Langton, Christopher. Artificial Life. In Artificial Life, Volume VI: SFI Studies in the Sciences of Complexity (Ed. C. Langton) Addison-Wesley, 1988.

15. Nonaka, Ikujiro and Takeuchi, Hirotaka. 1995. *The Knowledge Creating Company: How Japanese Companies Create the Dynamics of Innovation*, Oxford University Press.

16. Ogunnaike, B. 1994. *Process Dynamics, Modeling, and Control*. Oxford University Press.

17. Pittman, Matthew. Lessons Learned in Managing Object-Oriented Development. IEEE Software, January, 1993, pp. 43-53.

18. Rumbaugh, October 1995, "What Is a Method". Journal of Object Oriented Programming.

19. Schwaber, Ken. "Controlled Chaos: Living on the Edge." American Programmer, April 1996.

20. Sutherland, Jeff. ScrumWeb Home Page: A Guide to the SCRUM Development Process. Jeff Sutherland's Object Technology Web Page, 1996 <http://www.tiac.net/users/jsuth/scrum/index.html>

21. Takeuchi, Hirotaka and Nonaka, Ikujiro. January-February 1986. "The New New Product Development Game." Harvard Business Review.

APPENDIX 1: System Development Methodologies : Defined or Empirical

System development is the act of creating a logical construct that is implemented as logic and data on computers. The logical construct consists of inputs, processes, and outputs, both macro (whole construct) and micro (intermediate steps within whole construct). The whole is known as an implemented system.

Many artifacts are created while building the system. Artifacts may be used to guide thinking, check completeness, and create an audit trail. The artifacts consist of documents, models, programs, test cases, and other deliverables created prior to creating the implemented system. When available, a *metamodel* defines the semantic content of model artifacts. *Notation* describes the graphing and documentation conventions that are used to build the models.

The approach used to develop a system is known as a *method*. A *method* describes the activities involved in defining, building, and implementing a system; a *method* is a framework. Since a *method* is a logical process for constructing systems (process), it is known as a *metaprocess* (a process for modeling processes).

A *method* has micro and macro components. The macro components define the overall flow and time-sequenced framework for performing work. The micro components include *general design rules*, *patterns* and *rules of thumb*. *General design rules* state properties to achieve or to avoid in the design or general approaches to take while building a system. *Patterns* are solutions that can be applied to a type of development activity; they are solutions waiting for problems that occur during an activity in a method. *Rules of thumb* consist of a general body of hints and tips.

Figure 1 visualizes the relationship between the Method, the Artifacts, and the System.

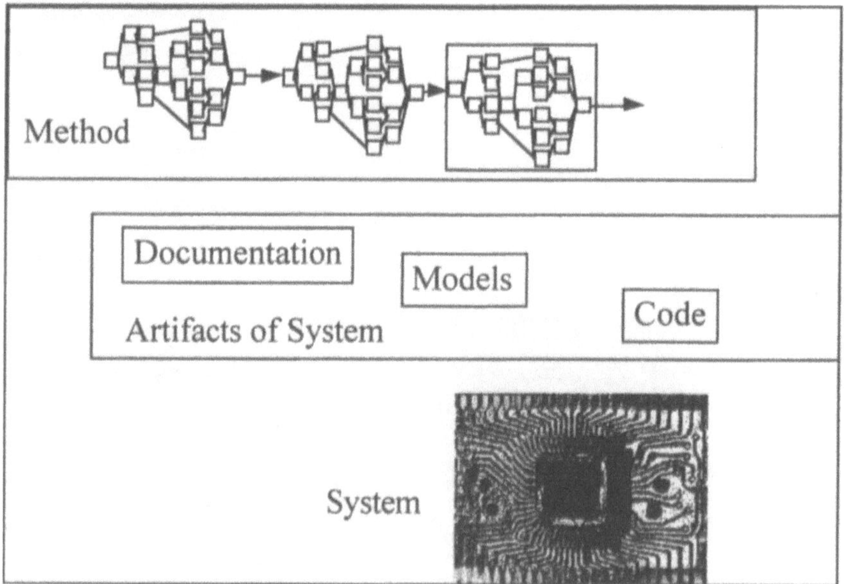

Figure 1: Relationship between the Method, the Artifacts, and the System

Applying concepts from industrial process control to the field of systems development, *methods* can be categorized as either "theoretical" (fully defined) or "empirical" (black box).

Correctly categorizing systems development methods is critical. The appropriate structure of a *method* for building a particular type of system depends on whether the method is theoretical or empirical.

Models of *theoretical processes* are derived from *first principles*, using material and energy balances and fundamental laws to determine the model. For a systems development *method* to be categorized as theoretical, it must conform to this definition.

Models of ***empirical processes*** are derived categorizing observed inputs and outputs, and defining controls that cause them to occur within prescribed bounds. Empirical process modeling involves constructing a process model strictly from experimentally obtained input/output data, with no recourse to any laws concerning the fundamental nature and properties of the system. No *a priori* knowledge about the process is necessary (although it can be helpful); a system is treated like a black box.

Primary characteristics of both theoretical and empirical modeling are detailed in Table 1.

Theoretical Modeling	Empirical Modeling
1. Usually involves fewer measurements; requires experimentation only for the estimation of unknown model parameters.	Requires extensive measurements, because it relies entirely on experimentation for the model development.
2. Provides information about the internal state of the process.	Provides information only about that portion of the process which can be influenced by control action.
3. Promotes fundamental understanding of the internal workings of the process.	Treats the process like a "black box."
4. Requires fairly accurate and complete process knowledge.	Requires no such detailed knowledge; only that output data be obtainable in response to input changes.
5. Not particularly useful for poorly understood and/or complex processes.	Quite often proves to be the only alternative for modeling the behavior of poorly understood and/or complex processes.
6. Naturally produces both linear and nonlinear process models.	Requires special methods to produce nonlinear models.

Table 1: Primary Characteristics of Theoretical and Empirical Modeling.

Upon inspection, we assert that the systems development process is empirical:

1. Applicable first principles are not present
2. The process is only beginning to be understood
3. The process is complex
4. The process is changing

Most methodologists agree with this assertion; "...you can't expect a *method* to tell you everything to do. Writing software is a creative process, like painting or writing or architecture... ... (a *method*) supplies a framework that tells how to go about it and identifies the places where creativity is needed. But you still have to supply the creativity...."[14]

Categorizing the systems development methods as empirical is critical to the effective management of the systems development process.

If systems development *methods* are categorized as *empirical*, measurements and controls are required because it is understood that the inner workings of the *method* are so loosely defined that they cannot be counted on to operate predictably.

---

[14] James Rumbaugh, October 1995, "What Is a Method"., Object Journal

In the past, *methods* have been provided and applied as though they were theoretical. As a consequence, measurements were not relied upon and controls dependent upon the measurements weren't used.

Many of the problems in developing systems have occurred because of this incorrect categorization. When a black box process is treated as a fully defined process, unpredictable results occur. Also, the controls are not in place to measure and respond to the unpredictability.

In practice, at multiple companies over multiple projects within some companies, SCRUM has been observed to provide a viable solution these problems. Projects are delivered on time and often exceed the expectations of both users and management. While working on a SCRUM development team is intense, developers are rewarded by high team spirit, a deep sense of accomplishment, and a feeling that development can be an enjoyable and satisfying experience.

Experiences with a Manufacturing Framework

S. L. Stewart and James A. St. Pierre
U.S. DEPARTMENT OF COMMERCE[1]
Technology Administration
National Institute of Standards and Technology
Gaithersburg MD 20899 USA
Email: sstewart@nist.gov, james.st.pierre@nist.gov

ABSTRACT: *This paper describes the first year of a joint project between the National Institute of Standards and Technology (NIST) and SEMATECH. After studying the SEMATECH CIM Framework, we present a roadmap for adoption and use of manufacturing frameworks with four components: developing a specification, reaching consensus, standardization, and testing and certification. Results of our study include numerous recommendations about online specifications, supplier involvement, standards organizations, usage scenarios, reference implementations, and a testing and certification plan.*

KEY WORDS: *Application Framework; Certification; Computer Integrated Manufacturing; CORBA IDL; Standards; Testing*

1. Introduction

This paper is based on the report, *Roadmap for the Computer Integrated Manufacturing (CIM) Framework,* (Stewart and St. Pierre, 1995) for the first year of a joint project between the National Institute of Standards and Technology (NIST) and SEMATECH[2] under a Cooperative Research and Development Agreement (CRADA) between the two organizations.

SEMATECH developed a framework for CIM applications (SEMATECH, 1995), the CIM Application Framework, based on work by Texas Instruments (TI), a member company, in their Microelectronics Manufacturing Science and Technology (MMST) project. The goals of this CIM Framework are to promote integration on the shop floor, reduce costs, and increase reuse through object-oriented technology. The CIM Framework is based on the Object Management Group's (OMG) Common Object Request Broker Architecture (CORBA). In particular the specification of the framework uses the OMG interface definition language (IDL) to define the classes (interfaces) of the framework. In addition to IDL test, the specification uses Harel state charts and Rumbaugh diagrams, as well as English narrative.

---

[1]Official contribution of the National Institute of Standards and Technology; not subject to copyright in the United States.

[2]This work was supported jointly by SEMATECH contract #34008401 and by NIST under its Scientific and Technical Research and Services budget.

We were asked to study the CIM Framework with respect to two broad areas: (1) Generalization, Standardization, and Promotion, and (2) Conformance Testing and Certification. Our work was based primarily on version 1.1 of the SEMATECH specification. The latest version, 1.2, is available and a subsequent version is in preparation. There are many improvements and corrections in the later versions, but for the broad subjects discussed in this paper the version number is not significant.

Here we present some of our results for a more general audience about the adoption, use, standardization, testing, and certification of the SEMATECH CIM Framework[3]. It is our belief that this paper is valuable precisely because much of what we learned is applicable to other manufacturing frameworks. Neither the publication of this paper nor our original report should be taken as endorsement or acceptance by SEMATECH of any of the recommendations or conclusions.

2. Generalization, Standardization, and Promotion

2.1. Roadmap

A roadmap to standardization for a CIM Framework goes through several stages. The analogy to a roadmap is only loosely true because the stages are overlapping and most of the activities need to be carried out in parallel. However, the emphasis and level of effort will shift as we progress through this process. The principal stages are: specification, consensus, standardization, and testing/certification. Each of these stages is expanded below.

2.1.1. Specification

The logical first step in developing a standard framework is to create a specification. For the CIM Application Framework, this process started with the MMST project at Texas Instruments and is now being carried out by the Manufacturing Execution Systems (MES) Build Team at SEMATECH. The first version was published by SEMATECH on March 31, 1994, as *Collaborative Manufacturing System Computer Integrated Manufacturing (CIM) Application Framework Specification 1.0.* This was revised, and version 1.1 was published on August 31, 1994. The current version is 1.2 (SEMATECH, 1995), and version 2.0 is under development.

Our project took the electronic version of the original specification and converted it into a HTML document suitable for online browsing, that is, we made it a World Wide Web readable document. HTML, short for Hypertext Markup Language, is the specialization of SGML (Standard Generalized Markup Language, ISO 8879) used by Web servers for formatting compound documents. We subsequently updated the online version to 1.1. In so doing, we demonstrated the

---

[3]Certain commercial products are identified in this paper. These identifications are for clarity of presentation only. In no case does such identification imply recommendation or endorsement by the National Institute of Standards and Technology, nor does it imply that the products are among the best available for the purposes they serve.

feasibility of making the specification available in browsable, electronic form without having to distribute the original electronic document. John O'Connor and Fred Waskiewicz, from SEMATECH, were instrumental in making this conversion possible.

We recommend that this process be carried even further by planning for a future version of the specification in which one electronic source can be used to create three different forms of the specification: (1) the hardcopy version for printing, (2) an HTML version for online browsing, and (3) an extract of the formal portions of the specification for computer processing. We refer to this concept as single source specification management.

2.1.2. Consensus

To achieve SEMATECH's objectives, it is not sufficient to produce a specification, even one of technical excellence. There must also be widespread agreement among both the suppliers and users of manufacturing software that applications should be based on the specification. This consensus is a necessary step in the road to adoption and success.

SEMATECH has already involved the users' groups from its member companies in the process of developing the specification. It is also contacting independent suppliers and providing orientation and training about the CIM Framework in scheduled classes and public conferences. We believe that this process of awareness, involvement, and training is absolutely essential to the success of a CIM Framework, and we recommend that it be continued and expanded to the limits of the resources available.

2.1.3. Standardization

Standardization is the next step beyond consensus; it records the consensus in a well-defined and public way. Standards can be promulgated by national and international standards bodies or by groups of interested parties or by companies through widely used products.

The American National Standards Institute, a non-governmental organization, is the U.S. national standards body; however, many of its standards are developed by accredited standards development organizations (SDO), like the Institute for Electrical and Electronics Engineers (IEEE). At the international level there are several standards bodies, for example, the International Organization for Standardization (ISO) and the International Electrotechnical Commission (IEC). These bodies develop standards through technical committees of volunteer experts, but the final adoption is by ballot of the member countries.

Recently, there has been increased use of other kinds of organizations to develop standards in information technology where the pace of technical development is faster than traditional standards-making procedures can accommodate. Typically a consortium or similar organization will be formed to develop a specific technological area where consensus on standards is essential to creating the market for the new technology. One important example is the Object Management Group (OMG). It was organized in 1989 to develop an Object Management Architecture (OMA) and a Common Object Request Broker Architecture (CORBA).

SEMATECH is a corporate member of OMG and has committed to using CORBA as the basis for binding CIM Framework-conformant applications to a computing infrastructure. The formal syntax for the interfaces is specified in CORBA Interface Definition Language (IDL). It is these IDL interface specifications that comprise the computer processible portions that would be extracted from the single source specification recommended above. These same specifications can be the basis for submission of a CIM Framework to the OMG Technical Committee (TC) as part of a vertical market CORBA common facility for manufacturing.

2.1.4. Testing and Certification

A CIM Framework will not be a success if it is not used, and standardization is only one step in raising users' confidence to that point. Another important step in the quality assurance process is to have some means of testing implementations for conformance to the standard and a certification process to attest to the results. This topic was a principal study area for this project, and the results are discussed in detail in Section 3 below.

2.2. Significant Issues

In this section we briefly identify a number of issues that can have an important influence on the success of a CIM Framework. In some cases there are specific recommendations. However, we believe that all these issues warrant continued attention for the life of the project.

2.2.1. Supplier Involvement and Support

Earlier we identified supplier involvement as critical to the success of a CIM Framework. Unless the suppliers of manufacturing software adopt the CIM Framework, this work may have great technical value, but it will not bring about the cost and productivity benefits expected. As much as 70% of the cost of semiconductor manufacturing software, and especially the integration costs, are generated by in-house software groups of the manufacturer. So, the semiconductor manufacturer is typically both a user and a supplier. When the manufacturer contracts out the systems integration, then a third party integration company also becomes part of the supplier chain.

This diversity of suppliers becomes even more complicated when a CIM Framework is generalized to a broader manufacturing community where each type of manufacturing may have its own segment-specific software supplier chain. This means that we need to identify and work with trade associations and consortia to reach as many suppliers as possible.

2.2.2. Formal Specification

We very much support the use of formal description techniques (FDT) in the specification. A CIM Framework is intended to be a standard for software development, that is, for creating computer programs and their data. Computer programs are, in their own way, the ultimate in formal specification. But, they are too detailed for many kinds of human analysis. Therefore the goal of a framework or other high-level specification is to capture as much of the essence as possible, while suppressing the implementation details and maintaining the benefits of formal description.

The IDL portions of the specification are central to the success of a CIM Framework in the CORBA environment, and they are a good example of the benefits of FDT. However, IDL is only intended to capture the signatures of the method interfaces, essentially a syntactic specification. In order to fully characterize the methods, we need to capture their semantics as well. Lawrence Eng, at SEMATECH, is making a valuable contribution by exploring VDM++ as a semantic specification technique, and we plan to leverage that work into the development of test implementations of applications.

In the CIM Framework, semantics are captured in a combination of English narrative, Rumbaugh diagrams, and Harel state charts. While the last two are formal, they are essentially graphical or tabular and not easily converted for automatic computer manipulation. There are many FDTs to choose among; so, there will be problems when one formally specified framework is integrated with the work of other groups that have independently chosen a different FDT. At present it does not seem likely that one FDT will become dominant; so this will likely remain a significant integration issue at the enterprise level.

A second potential problem is that FDT tools include their own definition of signatures covered by IDL. In order to use both, a way must be found to harmonize the mappings defined by CORBA for IDL with the mappings defined by tools associated with a semantic FDT.

Despite these potential problems, the benefits of FDTs are sufficient to recommend their use.

2.2.3. Evolution and Maintenance of the Specification

The SEMATECH specification and most other contemporary specifications are essentially traditional paper documents. Even though modern electronic document preparation technology is used to maintain a master version, the form is still one of a carefully prepared paper publication. In this respect it is like almost every other formal standard.

As we discussed in Section 2.1.1 we propose going a step further by making the electronic form itself the master version while doing it in such a way that equivalent versions of the specification can be produced for specific needs with a high degree of automation. This does not negate the change control process in any way although it may make the updating of changes easier. There is often a significant ripple effect when one change forces changes elsewhere in the document. A carefully constructed electronic hypertext document can make this updating simpler, and in some cases automatic.

There are several other recommendations to make any specification more manageable and useful:

Partition the specification. A specification proper is often the bulk of the formal document, but there is much introductory and explanatory material that must be included. The specification will also be the part that changes most rapidly and the part most useful in machine-processible form.

Separating it from the rest of the document would facilitate maintenance.

Develop usage scenarios. There are many places in interface definitions where the intentions of the designers are often ambiguous to outside readers, particularly as to whether an interface is supposed to cause a change in state or to record that a state has changed. Detailed scenarios of how some of the important interfaces are intended to be used would resolve the question for those not directly involved in the formulation and evolution of the specification.

Use IDL *modules* to control name scope. IDL has the concept of modules to control the scope of names (identifiers). These modules are not only useful as a software development tool, but also avoid potential problems of name collision when changes are made to other parts of the specification.

Use CORBAfacilities and CORBAservices. The OMG Common Facilities and Common Services have been renamed, but they are still being actively developed to extend the range of functions defined by CORBA. Incorporating existing specifications is the epitome of reuse.

2.3. Technical Recommendations

In the process of studying this specification and other IDL specifications, for example, the National Industrial Information Infrastructure Protocols (NIIIP) reference architecture and several of the proposals to OMG, we have come to a number of conclusions about a style for writing IDL. Here we present some of the most important conclusions in a series of recommendations about how to write specifications of this kind.

2.3.1. Parameters

Avoid 'inout' Parameters. Only use 'inout' where it is absolutely necessary and it should never be necessary. Do not use it to avoid inventing another parameter name. In fact all parameters should be grouped into the 'in' parameters first, followed by the 'out' parameters, if any. This should always be possible because the IDL is based on a message passing paradigm, where the 'in' parameters are the request message, and the 'out' parameters plus the method value are the response message.

Use meaningful, but brief, parameter names. IDL is primarily a syntax specification. The small amount of semantics available in IDL is contained in the agreed upon (standard) types, the structure of **typedefs**, and whatever connotation is provided by the choice of names. It is impossible to be formal, or even rigorous, in specifying semantics through names alone; so, do not try too hard by using long, convoluted name, for example, **top-leftmost-branch-of-the-call-tree-if-there-is-one**. On the other hand do not be deliberately obtuse by using names like **astring** or **value1**.

Use 'readonly' wherever possible. 'Readonly' has two possible uses depending on exactly how the IDL is meant. One possibility is that it specifies an attribute that must be set at create-time, meaning that it is essential to the identity of the object and cannot be changed: there is no _set method. If an error is made in one of these values at creation, the only recourse is to destroy the object and create anew. This is a very important feature and is analogous to the key field(s) in a relational database. The other possible use of 'readonly' (where multiple interfaces are allowed) is to restrict the attribute in question, in that interface, to be retrievable but not modifiable. In database terminology, this is called a view. Such a feature can have value for both performance optimization and security controls. It should be noted that CORBA does not allow multiple interfaces at this time, but it is a subject of debate.

2.3.2. Exceptions

Almost any method may raise an exception of some sort. If nothing else there might have been a hardware, software, or communications failure while the method was executing. Section 4.14 of CORBA 1.2 (Chapter 4 of *The Common Object Request Broker: Architecture and Specification*, document 93-12-43 on the OMG server) covers the standard exceptions provided by CORBA. These exceptions cover most possible failure modes, and a conforming application will need to handle these exceptions.

For one important set of objects, we believe that all exceptions are handled by the standard exceptions. This is the set of data-centric objects that are made up of _get methods (or _get and _set if the attribute is not 'readonly'). The same argument applies to other retrieval methods whether they are simple _get's or not. And the same rule can be applied even if the method is computational, if no non-standard exceptions can occur. No new exceptions need to be defined but the standard exceptions must be processed correctly.

Now to the case where there are truly non-standard exceptions possible. We use the word 'exception' rather than 'error' because there are many more interesting cases where exceptions are a normal but alternative response. For example, suppose a program requests an agent-object to perform some service. In processing the request, the agent concludes that although it cannot respond exactly to the original request, there is an alternative that might do the job, but the response is very different in structure. Raising an exception is the method of choice in IDL for returning a significantly different signature.

2.3.3. Returning Values

Defining exceptions is one of the weaker points of the current specification. We believe that the specification can be significantly improved by reviewing the values returned by the methods and adding exceptions where needed. Based on the discussion in the previous section, we can catalog object methods pragmatically into four categories based on how exceptions are used:

No non-standard exceptions. Return result, or if the result is more complex, return a main result as the value of the method and other results as 'out' parameters. They should be 'out' only, not 'inout'.

Simple, two-valued exception. A success/fail response is common to many methods. Return a Boolean, and the actual results as 'out' parameters. This assumes that no additional information needs to be returned in the false case.

More than two modes of return. If the results have the same signature in every case, or are a subset (possibly empty), of the 'normal' return, then return an **enum value** from an **enum type** defined for this method, or a set of methods that share the same possible modes of return. This situation arises often in the specification where the state of a process is being queried or set. The specification uses numerous Boolean methods to report each state separately. By combining all these state-reporting functions into a single method that returns an **enum value**, the specification is not only much simpler to read and understand, but easier to modify. Even a structured state can be returned by only two or three methods, one for each partition of the state structure.

The most complex case. Where the 'normal' response and the 'exceptional' responses can be quite different, the programmer (method designer) will need to create one or more user-defined exceptions. This is also one of the few cases where a 'void' return might be appropriate. Think very carefully before invoking this heavy-duty machinery.

3. Testing and Certification

3.1. Introduction

A few definitions are in order:
    Conformance: To be in accordance with some specified standard or specification.
    Certification: A procedure by which a third party gives written assurance that a product, process, or service conforms to specific requirements.

One of the most critical aspects of a certification program is having it be accepted by the industry, and primarily the suppliers since they are most directly affected by the program. The suppliers should be involved from the very beginning of definition of the certification program in order to ensure the its success.

In general it is recommended that the details of the certification program (business model and methodology) be defined as early as possible in the development process. This report reviews various models for certification programs and makes recommendations for the approach to be taken with regard to a CIM Framework.

A CIM Framework specification is understood to be a work in progress and is evolving as expected with new levels of detail at each revision. The addition of formal definitions, to describe the behavior of the framework, will greatly assist the certification program development, in that the expected behavior will be more rigorously defined. Also formal descriptions lend themselves to automated test generation techniques. In addition the development of a reference implementation is strongly recommended to aid in the successful development of a certification program.

3.1.1. Defining Interoperability Goals

It is reasonable to ask the question, "what is the point of certification?" It is not just assurance of some level of *quality*. Usually certification conjures up notions of compatibility, interoperability, and portability (Mallis, 1995). In industry today, interoperability tests often refer to the testing, via pairwise matching, of specific supplier applications. This is a very expensive proposition especially as the number of applications to be certified increases.

In some cases, the certification of the application program interfaces (API) themselves provides a high level of interoperability. POSIX is a case in point. There is no explicit interoperability certification involved in the POSIX certification. However, one of the results of POSIX certification is the ability for different Unix implementations to interoperate at certain levels. This is due to the fact that the POSIX standard itself provides good coverage of the domain for which it is intended.

Interoperability or compatibility are loose terms that suggest some kind of cooperation or harmony among unlike components of a system. These terms have been applied to features ranging from "is written in the same language" to "can read ASCII" to "plug-and-play." Portability is often mentioned when defining interoperability goals, and it usually means the ability to move a program or piece of data around among different environments and still be able to use it with a minimum of effort, even though the program may be very unlike other components in design or function. "Usually, the tighter the integration required to satisfy interoperability requirements, the more cost and effort involved. Real-life compromises will reflect acceptable thresholds of pain for integrators." (Mallis, 1995)

For example, even perfect POSIX conformance still will not guarantee that an application will compile the first time on a foreign system. But compared to the problems of Unix porting in the past, these problems are considered minor, and do not detract from the usefulness of the POSIX standard in promoting portability. This should be understood in the context of a CIM framework. Even if the framework does not provide perfect interoperability, it can still be successful if it provides a noticeable net decrease in integration costs.

In the current CIM Framework specification it is not clear as to whether the primary goal is to promote and provide some level of re-use or whether the main focus is on interoperability. Our recommendation would be that the main focus should be on interoperability, and that re-use be considered a valuable side-effect of the specification. Enforcing good OO (object-oriented) programming practices on developers is neither practical nor useful. If a supplier can provide a product that passes certification at the component interface level, then it is irrelevant how the product is actually implemented. The focus should be on the plug-and-play aspect of interoperability with respect to the semiconductor manufacturing floor. However, it is very useful to educate the developers about the tremendous benefits available via the use of object-oriented technology.

The reference implementation is critical in order to provide some initial CIM Framework services and simple applications, which suppliers' products may be tested against. The key here is not only to develop a robust reference implementation, but to also develop detailed scenarios which exercise a wide range of application interaction.

3.2. Business Case for Certification Testing

One of the first things that should be decided when designing a test plan for a specification is who will pay for certification? Certification or the issuing of a certificate is actually the final step in the process. The creation of a full certification program will require several different steps, the main four ones being:
1. Test suite development
2. Testing service procedures and execution
   (may include accreditation procedures for third party labs)
3. Maintenance of the test suite
4. Administration and issuing of certificates

There are several potential methods for funding:

Consortium pays

Example: VHDL members put in funds and resources and contracted with a university to develop the conformance test suite. SEMATECH could fund the effort initially and plan to migrate support of the program to another organization.

Suppliers or customers pay

Example: the CAD Framework Initiative (CFI) charges for its certification service for its Design Representation (DR) standard. The cost is either absorbed by the supplier requesting the certification or passed along to the final customer in the price of the product.

Public organization pays for development of a certification program

Example: the SQL test suite and certification program was developed by NIST. However, even if this method is used to develop the initial program, there should be a long-term plan to make the program self-sufficient.

Independent company develops the test suite

Example: Perenial, Inc. developed the C programming language test suite. There was no direct payment to Perenial, however NIST (the certification authority in this case) had an agreement with Perenial to recognize their C test suite for conformance testing.

In the SEMATECH case, the consortial approach is recommended because it would spread the initial cost over most major users. SEMATECH could provide this funding, which could entitle member companies to discounted certification. The idea would be for SEMATECH to explore other funding sources to maintain the program.

3.2.1. Selling Certification

Certification is a marketable service and must be promoted like any product or service. As in any marketing effort the benefits of using the product or service must be clearly presented to the target audience. For example, the approach used with a company which supplies tools to semiconductor manufacturers may be somewhat different from the approach used with information systems (IS) people within a semiconductor manufacturer. Suppliers wish to sell more of their products and services, whereas IS people want to be able to integrate new tools quickly into their manufacturing line. It can be the case that suppliers are fearful of open standards. This is because open standards are intended to prevent a supplier from holding a customer hostage within a proprietary environment. This attitude needs to be understood in order to effectively convince the suppliers that the benefits of certification to an open standard outweigh any negative side effects. Some of the benefits are decreased time to market, reduced development costs, improved quality by leveraging off of test suites, and increasing the potential market, in addition to:

- Easier entry into previously *closed* shops, by virtue of being able to introduce a small piece rather than a complete solution, that is, plug-and-play provides a mechanism for a supplier to get their foot in the door more easily. In general it is easier to convince a customer to try a small piece of your solution. Rather than starting at ground zero with your products, you can introduce them slowly to help a customer migrate to your tools.

- In companies which have decentralized purchasing, different manufacturing sites can easily purchase different tools to suit their specific requirements. Of course large companies may want to take advantage of volume purchase agreements, but a CIM Framework makes it much easier for them to do it with multiple vendors.

- Suppliers may be able to deliver products sooner, since the plug-and-play nature of a CIM Framework allows finer-grain resolution on integrating new tools into the line. This has the result of effectively shortening the development cycle and introducing products in phases.

- Customers are more receptive to buying certified products.

- Successful completion of the certification program can result in gaining insight and experience in quality issues that can be reapplied in other company development processes.

- Inclusion of a supplier's products in various announcements or listings of conformant applications, provides additional marketing which can generate new sales for a supplier. Some of the means of disseminating this information are: press releases, trade journals, Usenet news groups, the World Wide Web, or a formal registry.

For example, Novell circulates a test bulletin (via their YES source book, NetWare support encyclopedia, NetWire, Reseller News, and the IMSP index) to inform the industry about a product's Tested and Approved status. CFI maintains current lists of certified products, as well as interactive demonstrations on the World Wide Web. They also circulate press releases to appropriate channels, and have a ready-made network of key industry contacts by virtue of their position as a consortium (Mallis, 1995).

Developing test suites can be incredibly expensive. For example, here are some rough estimates of the effort expended developing certification test suites for some common languages, at the API level (where a test suite is a collection of individual test cases).

Table 1 Certification Test Suite Effort Levels

146

Specification	Estimated effort (Person Years) for certification test suite development
FORTRAN	9-10
VHDL	9-10
COBOL	10-15
POSIX	10-11
C	4-5
SQL	10+

Note that this only addresses API level testing and does not include any interoperability testing of various implementations of the above specifications working with multiple implementations.

Because of the similarity between POSIX procedure calls and CIM Framework methods, we can estimate the effort needed to develop certification for a CIM Framework. The number of procedure calls in POSIX can be compared to the number of methods in a CIM Framework. There are approximately 250 procedure calls in the POSIX standard. There are 3000 tests in the POSIX test suite. From this we can estimate 3000/250 = 12 tests per procedure call. In the CIM Framework specification there are approximately 770 unique methods. If we use the POSIX model we can estimate the number of tests per method as 12, then 12x770 = 9240 tests for the CIM Framework. That is approximately three times the number of tests required for POSIX, which would give an estimate of 3 x (9 to 10) person-years or between 27 and 30 person-years of effort to code the test suite for API level testing of the CIM Framework. See section 3.4 below for recommendations to address the high cost of testing.

3.3. Methodology for Certification Testing

Another key question to be answered when defining a certification testing program is, "who will perform the test service?" First let us consider the three main phases which define the execution of a certification program. They are:

1. Research and development phase
    Test suite development
    Final test execution procedure definition
        Details for execution of certification tests
    Criteria for recognizing testing laboratories
        Accreditation and written agreements with laboratories (if used)
2. Testing phase
    Execution of testing according to procedures
    Generation of reports
3. Certification phase

Review of test reports
Issuing of certificate, adding to a registry, *etc.*

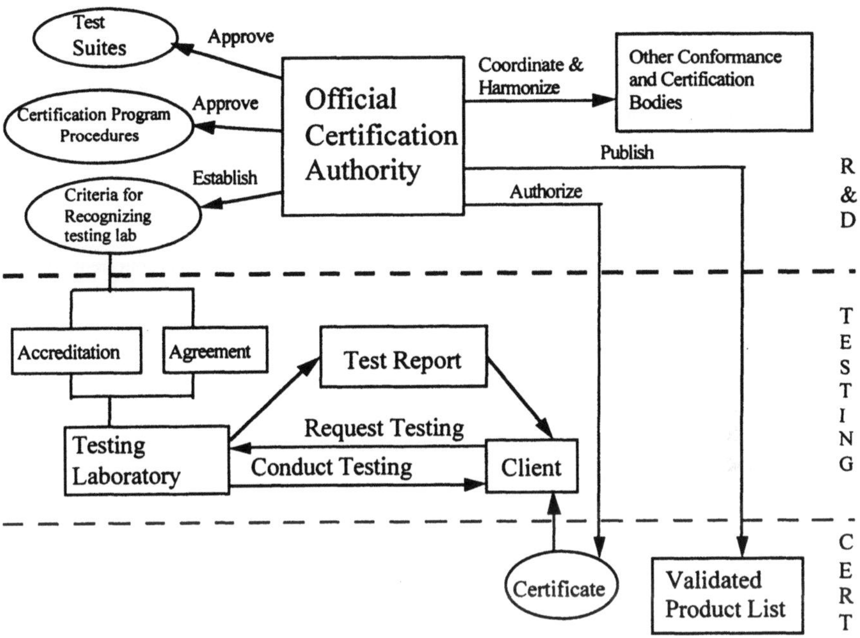

Figure 1 *Certification program components*

Figure 1 shows many of the tasks that might be involved in a certification program. Note that a given methodology may not incorporate every task in Figure 1. Note also that some tasks may be provided by more than one organization. For example, in the self-certification methodology described below, the testing laboratory task can be performed either by the supplier, or by the official certifying body, in the event of an audit.

One methodology sometimes referred to as *self-certification* requires the supplier to provide a test plan to the official certifying body. The certifying body reviews the test plan and recommends changes if necessary. Changes to the test plan are made until the certifying body approves the test plan. The supplier then executes the test plan against their product. The official certifying body reviews the results of the suppliers testing and delivers the certificate indicating the results. (See certificate contents). The official certifying body reserves the right (at any time and for any reason) to audit the test, or to require the performance of the tests in the presence of a representative of the certifying body. This is a preferred method because of the minimal cost and the benefits to suppliers. By using the provided test suites during development suppliers can improve both their quality and time to market. This aspect increases the appeal of the certification program to the suppliers.

Another methodology would use the services of an accredited testing laboratory, that is, a laboratory accredited through a formal laboratory accreditation program such as National Voluntary Laboratory Accreditation Program (NVLAP). The accredited laboratory would then execute the testing phase. This might involve a representative of the accredited laboratory visiting the supplier to supervise the execution of the appropriate tests. The accredited lab then sends the reports to the official certifying body. One of the issues with this approach is that the laboratory needs to maintain competency and be re-accredited periodically which can be costly. One of the advantages of this approach is that the testing is performed by an independent third party.

The Certificate itself should contain at least the following information:
- Procedures followed (may include a detailed test plan)
- Versions (and model numbers) of all relevant software and hardware components used during testing.
- Profiles of tests performed (For example, what CIM Framework components were tested?)
- Organization performing the testing
- Organization auditing the testing (if applicable)
- Evidence or reference to related standards conformance (as required)
- Overall Pass/Fail status

3.4. Summary of Recommendations on Testing

We strongly recommend that the suppliers be involved as soon as possible in the definition of the certification and conformance testing program. Without the suppliers' buy-in the program cannot succeed. This must take into account certifying legacy applications and fully compliant implementations. Giving the suppliers the certification test suites provides an incentive for them to take part in certification. The test suite would be expensive for any one of them to develop alone but will be extremely valuable to all of their quality assurance processes.

We strongly recommend that any requirement to have access to a supplier's source code be abandoned. Other certification programs have found that suppliers are extremely unwilling to provide access to their source code, since in most cases this is how they distinguish themselves in a competitive marketplace. All supplier product testing for the purposes of certification should be considered from a black box perspective, that is, without reference to the source code, only from the interfaces defined by the IDL in the specification.

We recommend that methods for automatically generating tests be explored further. There are research projects and companies that are focusing on this question. Interactive Development Environments (IDE), for example, has developed a tool which reads in IEEE Standard 1175 STL (Semantic Transfer Language) and automatically creates tests. Other research is being done on ADL (Assertion Definition Language). Any automation of test generation could provide tremendous savings in developing a certification program.

We recommend supplier involvement in test suite development to establish a consensus for the program. We also recommend investigating universities as a technical resource for manual and automatic test generation. This would also transfer knowledge of a CIM Framework to the next generation of engineers.

We recommend a self-certification program which is audited by SEMATECH. There are many advantages to the self-certification program; for example, it involves the suppliers and has benefits for them such as improvements in the quality assurance process.

We recommend leveraging off of existing standards, for example, requiring all communication to be CORBA conformant will greatly enhance the interoperability of the specification. Currently the specification discusses CORBA but never indicates that it is a requirement. The certification plan could then require CORBA conformance prior to CIM Framework certification. Also, pushing any common facilities into other standards efforts would off-load some effort from SEMATECH. An example of this might be that event management could be provided by CORBAfacilities.

We recommend that a document be generated which contains the assertions for the specification. This provides a formal document which defines what is to be tested and how. This is closely related to exploring automated methods of test generation from the formal specification.

4. Conclusions

Many of the recommendations made for the development of the CIM Framework are generally applicable to other object-oriented framework developments:

- Adopt a single source electronic specification management approach.
- Increase supplier involvement in both specification and certification development.
- Give a reference implementation high priority.
- Reach consensus on a certification business model and methodology as part of the specification development.
- Address the high cost of certification in the business plan.
- Develop usage scenarios to clarify the implementation and use of a framework.
- Build on existing specifications, such as, CORBAfacilities and CORBAservices.
- Do not make certification dependent on access to suppliers' source code.
- Focus on interoperability.
- Expand use of formal description techniques in specifications.
- Explore automatic test generation techniques.
- Require suppliers to provide certification tests for any extensions they add.

Acknowledgments: The work was carried out by a team at NIST led by the authors and including Neil Christopher, Elizabeth Fong, Barbara Goldstein, Greg Koeser, Tom Kramer, Michael McCaleb, Michael McLay, Steve Osella, and Evan Wallace. We also want to acknowledge valuable discussions with John Barkley, Ed Barkmeyer, Kevin Brady, Tony

Cincotta, Barbara Cuthill, Martha Gray, Shirley Hurwitz, Arnold Johnson, and Tom Rhodes. Valuable technical support was provided by Joe Chandler.

References:

David Mallis, *Final Draft Report on Compliance and Certification*, contractor report (unpublished) for contract 43NANB510468, National Institute of Standards and Technology, Gaithersburg MD 20899, 1995.

SEMATECH, *Computer Integrated Manufacturing (CIM) Application Framework Specification 1.2*, SEMATECH Technology Transfer #93061697E-ENG, Austin TX 78741-6499, 1995.

S. L. Stewart and James A. St. Pierre, *Roadmap for the Computer Integrated Manufacturing (CIM) Framework*, SEMATECH Technology Transfer #93061697E-ENG, Austin TX 78741-6499, 1995, also NISTIR 5679, National Institute of Standards and Technology, Gaithersburg MD 20899, 1995.

Business Application Components

Tom Digre

Business Application Components
Information Technology Group
Texas Instruments, Inc.
6620 Chase Oaks Blvd. MS: 8417
Plano, Texas 75023
e-mail:digre@ti.com fax: 214-575-2866

ABSTRACT. *Information Technology is being driven by the need for rapid provisioning of business solutions within an environment of increasing complexity. Component-based architecture principles and complexity-hiding model-based development techniques will empower users to dynamically change business processes, workflows, rules, policies, presentation, and other aspects of their environment.*

KEY WORDS: *component, development, architecture, semantics, complexity.*

1. Introduction

Global business competition and a shift from commodity to custom products has created an environment of continuous business structure change. In order to effectively compete, businesses are constantly revisiting products, processes, suppliers, and customer care-abouts. As shown in " Figure 1: Business Drivers", a primary business driver for Information Technology includes the profit-oriented objective to decrease time-to-market for products and services (Wirthman, 1995) within an environment of increasing business complexity (Martin, 1991) resulting from accelerating changes to products, processes, customers, partners, and Information Technology. A successful information strategy will accommodate these business drivers by provisioning business solutions at a rate commensurate with the increasing rate of business structural change.

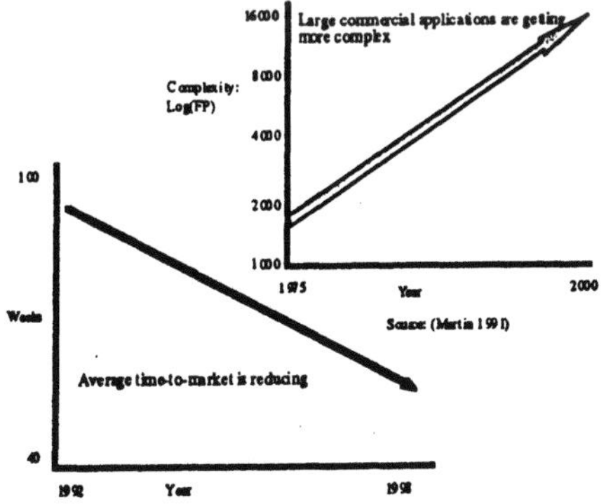

Figure 1: Business Drivers

152

Rapid solution delivery in response to continuous business process changes requires direct involvement of empowered users to dynamically change their business processes, workflows, rules, policies, presentation, and other aspects of their environment. Impediments to achieving these goals have been technological and organizational barriers between business and the enterprise's information technology. Enterprise IT organizations are on the critical path to achieving the IT productivity, performance, and cycle time gains necessary to support business change.

2. Coping with Complexity

IT organizations are severely challenged to meet the solution provisioning cycle time requirements imposed by business. These organizations are facing the dilemma of minimal software productivity improvements, particularly when using third generation languages such as COBOL, C++, and Smalltalk. A fundamental problem with software solutions implemented using 3GL is the inability to cope with increasing business complexity. As depicted in "Figure 2: Software Complexity", as complexity increases there is an adverse impact on productivity, quality, delivery cycle time, and cost (Martin, 1991).

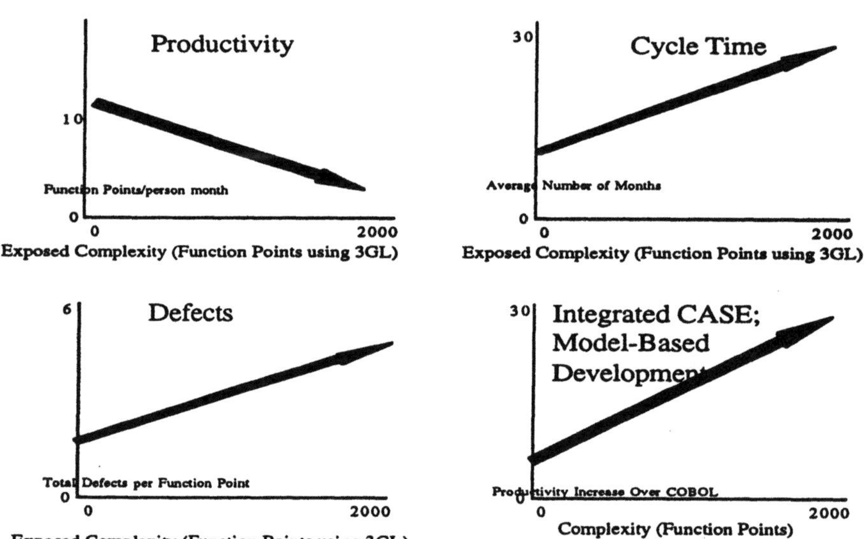

Figure 2: Software Complexity

Software productivity depends not only on sheer bulk but also on "surface area", the number of things that must be understood and properly dealt with in order to successfully enable interoperability between software components (Cox, 1987). Factors influencing surface area include:

- Amount of visible information. Surface area increases with the number of names that are exposed through the software component interface, including data element names, data types, and function names.

- Sequence dependencies. Surface area increases with each requirement that the software component user must perform operations in a particular order.

- Environment and responsibility scope dependencies. Surface area increases whenever the software component user is responsible for managing lifecycle, persistence, location, or environmental aspects of software components within a more global application context.
- Technology dependencies. Surface area increases with exposure to each technical domain and form of interface, including middleware communications, data storage.
- Concurrency. Surface area increases when concurrency issues are exposed to the software component user.

Use of third generation languages typically increase exposed "surface area" proportional to increases in underlying complexity. This is the fundamental problem: the complexity of the entire IT solution space, including the underlying IT infrastructure, is exposed to the solution provider. It is the exposed "surface area", not the underlying complexity, that impedes progress. Contrast software productivity with gains achieved in hardware componentization, as shown in "Figure 3: Need for Componentization Concepts". Hardware complexity has increased by nearly 2^{30} in the last 30 years, and it has been accomplished with minimal increase of surface area. While semiconductor (and downstream hardware) technology has consistently sustained an annual doubling of productivity and performance gains, significant software productivity gains have not materialized. Business application software continues to be characterized by surface area increases commensurate with complexity increases.

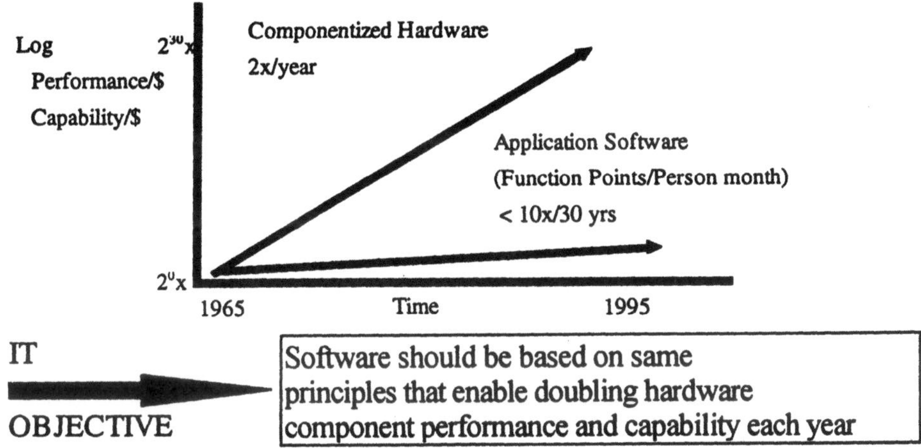

Figure 3: Need for Componentization Concepts

The success of the semiconductor industry to successfully manage complexity inspired Brad Cox to reflect on the potential for software componentization (as paraphrased from (Cox, 1987)):

Gordon Moore, the chairman of Intel Corporation, once predicted that the number of components on a silicon integrated chip would continue to double yearly. The prediction, now known as Moore's law, has held up remarkably well during the twenty years I've been in this business. One of its many implications is that during the same period that my productivity has been growing arithmetically with each improvement in programming language technology, the productivity of my friends in the hardware industry has been growing geometrically as the capability of the building blocks that they work with doubled each year for twenty years. My *productivity certainly improved in moving from assembly language to FORTRAN to C to Lisp. But it certainly did not improve by the million-fold increase implied by Moore's law: $2^{20} = 1,048,576$.*

Board designers routinely reuse the work of circuit designers, who reuse the efforts of workers at even lower levels - wafer manufacturers, mask fabricators, printing shops. Communication channels (trade magazines) allow suppliers to communicate with potential consumers, and consumers have catalogs, filing systems, performance tests, price comparisons for selecting among multiple suppliers. The impressive vitality of the marketplace in reusable hardware components is legendary.

The appeal of all this is the possibility that the software industry might obtain some of the benefits that the silicon chip brought to the hardware industry; the ability of a supplier to deliver a tightly encapsulated unit of functionality that is specialized for its intended function, yet independent of any particular application. The silicon chip is the unit of hardware reusability that has most conspicuously contributed to the hardware productivity boom. Might the Software-IC concept do the same for software?

Hardware IC componentization is an iterative process of encapsulating function, then using that function as the semantic basis for the next iteration of function delivery. Each iteration is starting at a higher conceptual level. The geometric function increase did not occur by going back to NAND gates, it occurred by raising the conceptual foundation for each iteration. The component user "assembles" the solution from increasingly sophisticated components to satisfy his unique engineering requirement. He assembles logical components directly into Application Specific Integrated Circuits. The resulting aggregate component has its function integrity maintained across the continual changes of infrastructure resulting from manufacturing process technology improvements. To protect both the consumer and the manufacturer, component reuse occurs at the design level and is critically dependent upon semantic clarity of exposed functionality.

Exploitation of these component concepts within the software domain will be aided by open standards for specification of component syntax and semantics; the existence of a marketplace (suppliers and consumers) for reusable software components; and tools for the construction of components and consequent assembly of components into solutions. Together, the component concept and supporting tools will enable the business user to:

- Directly provision his business solution.
- Express his specification in a form consistent with the problem domain.
- Focus "surface area" exposure on the business problem domain. All underlying technological and implementation complexity will be hidden.

Software is often viewed as creative technological "art" derived from solitary, mental, abstract activity akin to mathematics or novel writing. However, there is increasing consumer demand to establish manufacturing and engineering discipline in the production of software, driven by the need to build and use commercially robust repositories of trusted, stable components whose properties can be understood and tabulated in standard catalogs, like the handbooks of other mature engineering domains (Cox, 1990):

The denizens of the software domain, from the tiniest expression to the largest application, are as intangible as any ghost. And because we invent them all from first principles, everything we encounter there is unique and unfamiliar, composed of components that have never been seen before and will never be seen again, and that obey laws that don't generalize to future encounters. Software is a place where dreams are planted and nightmares harvested, an abstract, mystical swamp where terrible demons compete with magical panaceas, a world of werewolves and silver bullets. As long as all we can know for certain is the code we ourselves wrote during the last week or so, mystical belief will reign over quantifiable reason. Terms like `computer science' and `software engineering' will remain oxymorons -- at best, content-free twaddle spawned of wishful thinking and, at worst, a cruel and selfish fraud on the consumers who pay our salaries.

The `software industrial revolution' means ... transforming programming from a solitary cut-to-fit craft into an organizational enterprise like manufacturing. This means allowing consumers at every level of an organization to solve their own software problems as home owners solve plumbing problems: by assembling their own solutions from a robust commercial market in off-the-shelf subcomponents, which are in turn supplied by multiple lower level echelons of producers.

3. Component-based Solution Provisioning

A component-based IT architecture is founded on well-defined information components that can be specialized and/or assembled into applications. The architecture recognizes that components, including tools and services, can be purchased from external vendors (e.g., desktop tools); specialized and assembled by users (e.g., user-developed financial analysis); or developed by the IT provisioner. The component-based architecture defines the platform, or board, on which these reusable components can fit together.

Cycle time reduction goals require active participation by the business user. Ultimate cycle time reduction will occur when the business user is able to express his problem in a form consistent with his problem domain and have that specification automatically and instantly implemented. Building on component concepts and the need for solution provisioning directly by business users, an open component-based architecture will feature plug and play components and end-user empowerment. It is recognized that the goal of end-user solution provisioning will require cultural changes within the enterprise work force leading to a sharing of responsibility between the business user and the Information Technology provisioner.

Within the component-based architecture scenario, the business user will assume the responsibility for solution provisioning, as shown in "
Figure 4: Component-based Solution Provisioning". The role of solutions provisioning will migrate from the enterprise's Information Services organization to the business. The business user will be empowered to:

- Administrate business rules, work flows, and presentation.
- Specialize and assemble components into solutions using Enterprise modeling tools.

The Information Technology provisioner will provision reusable components that can be combined to form solutions by the business user. The IT provisioner will:

- Provision components through purchase, construction, or specialization and assembly of finer-grained components.
- Encapsulate purchased and legacy systems so they can be utilized as reusable, inter-operable components.
- Share Components with business users. The shared components include business rules, work flows, presentations, services, functions, and tools.

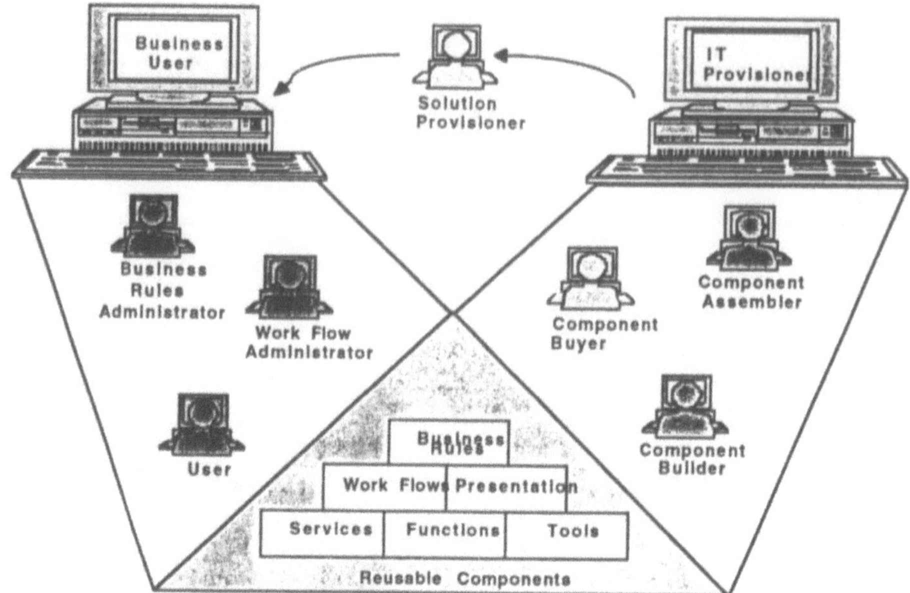

Figure 4: Component-based Solution Provisioning

All provisioning roles are inextricably tied to components. All roles specialize and assemble components. In most cases, the product of assembly is itself a reusable component. Cycle time reduction and business semantic integrity is ultimately dependent upon end-user assembly of these components.

When a business condition changes, the resulting modification to software is envisioned to occur only in those components directly associated with the changing business specification. Components will be loosely coupled, the impact of changes will be isolated to those components associated with the business semantic.

4. Component-based Architecture

A component-based architecture will help achieve the vision of business user solution provisioning. The component-based architecture shown in "
Figure 5: Component-based Architecture" is built upon layers of technology successively enabling capability on the path towards user-empowered solution assembly. The architectural structure is motivated by OMG-defined architectures [OMG 95.01.02, OMG 93.12.29, OMG 95.01.12] augmented with the concept of an **Enterprise Integration Model** that exposes relevant, domain-specific semantics of business application components to a suite of user empowerment tools.

The technology layers of the architecture include:

- **Platforms**, operating systems, database management systems, networks, and other fundamental software infrastructure components. This layer of technology currently enables rapid and transparent installation/replacement of tailorable infrastructure components within a broad range of reliability, performance, capacity, and price characteristics. These infrastructure components are no longer on the critical path to achieving objectives such as business solution cycle time reduction and end-user empowerment. Applications built directly on this layer are typically characterized as monolithic and centric.

- **ORB**(Object Request Broker). Using any of a variety of middleware communications mechanisms, this layer of technology typically enables construction of client/server applications founded on syntactic interoperability. CORBA is an example implementation [**OMG 93.12.29**]. The following features characterize components using this technology layer:
    - Implementation and location transparency. Clients are unaware of the location of server software components or their implementation details. Component implementation and location can change dynamically, without any modification to the client.
    - Universally accessible on federated enterprise ORBs.
    - Physical black-box encapsulation of related services.
    - Programming language independent. All component public interfaces are defined in IDL(Interface Definition Language).
    - Extensible, reusable specifications. Interface specifications can be inherited.
- **Object Services.** A set of fundamental services necessary to implement distributed applications. The services encompass distributed concepts of object relationships, concurrency, persistence, transactions, etc. [**OMG 95.01.12**]
- **Facilities.** Industrial adoption of a business component interoperability standard is on the critical path to definition and implementation of Business Application Components. A business component interoperability standard would enable specification of Business Application Components having the following characteristics:
    - Rigorous Semantics which enable plug-and-play, extensibility integrity, comprehension and control by business user.
    - Fully traceable life cycle, from business process engineering through deployment and continuing to final disposition.
- **Vertical Domains.** For each business domain, a set of plug and play Business Application Components compliant with industry-standard specifications. Industry standards are expected to evolve from activities of OMG Special Interest Groups and industrial consortia such as SEMATECH and OAG.
- **Enterprise Integration Model.** Provides for tailoring and integration of vertical domain components within an enterprise. Characterized by:
    - Context sensitivity, which enables domain-specific specification while maintaining cross-domain integrity and integration within the enterprise.
    - Complexity-hiding views which aid the process of empowering business users to directly provision their solutions.
    - Reuse through concepts of abstraction context inheritance, model-based specifications, and synthesis.
    - Versionable configurations of components.
- **Business User Empowerment.** A suite of tools interoperating with the **Enterprise Integration Model,** including business rule tools, work flow tools, presentation tools, software assembly tools, data access tools, and integrated CASE tools.

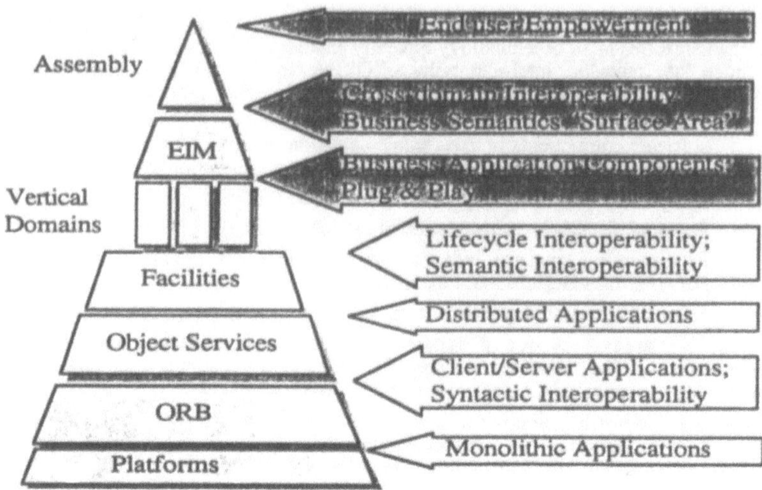

Figure 5:   **Component-based Architecture**

5. Model-based Development

The goals of the component-based architecture include:

- Business Semantic Integrity
- Rapid provisioning of business solutions;
- Reduction of "surface area".

These goals are coupled with an environment of increasing complexity in the areas of:

- Business.
- Technology.
- Architecture. The component-based architecture which has been outlined has, perhaps, orders of magnitude more implementation complexity than contemporary application architectures.

As discussed in the "2.   Coping with **Complexity**" section, there is a need to identify principles which would enable geometric productivity gains in software provisioning. Such gains are plausible using a model-based development approach. Such an approach would handle increasing complexity with minimal gain of surface area. The basic principle is to iteratively utilize generic constructs formulated at one level of abstraction as the "language" and semantic for the next level of specialization.

The complexities of using Object Services directly from 3GL code will be prohibitive for most application development organizations. Consequently, model-based development will practically become a necessity above the "ORB" layer of the architecture, and will likely encompass all architectural layers. Although model-based development is applicable to all architectural layers, the "Enterprise Integration Model" encompasses the most demanding aspects of model based development.

The (conceptual) Enterprise Integration Model (EIM) requires a set of tightly coupled concepts to support Business Application Component Engineering. Some of the concepts of EIM are reflected in conventional OO methodologies and toolsets. However, even for those few concepts which are conventionally available, the current implementations are disjoint, incomplete, and lack automation, rigor, consistency and integrity. Model-based development at the Enterprise Integration Model layer include the following, largely orthogonal, concepts:

- Life cycle
- Behavior
- Relations
- Specialization
- Context
- Genericity
- Version
- View

5.1. Life Cycle

The concept of life cycle encompasses a set of inter-related activities and artifacts related to Business Application Components. The life cycle is generally partitioned into the following "phases", but this should not necessarily imply that a "waterfall" lifecycle is being advocated:

- Business Process Engineering
- Analysis
- Design
- Implementation
- Construction
- Deployment
- Transition

Business Application Component Provisioning will generally be performed using the following life cycle strategies [OMG 92.10.01]:

- Non-staged, knowledge-based development. This approach does not place any management controls over the sequence of steps and their placement within stages. The steps are performed in any sequence, but the work is always constrained by the knowledge-base (rules of the method). For example the rules may prevent the recording of an operation unless it can be attached to an object type; or may define what constitutes a complete and correct object definition.
- Additive progression. Each stage adds more objects and more details to the model or design produced in the previous stage. This enables concurrent stage development, maintains traceability, avoids artificial "brick walls" between stages, and minimizes re-work when changes are needed in earlier stages. This approach avoids transformational strategies (including manual transformations). Note that a transformation may still be needed to "generate" the code and database designs of the production system. Enactable specifications are used during development to enable direct and immediate execution of designs.
- Incremental implementation. The underlying infrastructure, in conjunction with the EIM, enable incremental implementation of business application components and semantics. For example, adding new relationships (and enforced referential integrity) between components should be implementable without modification to any of the participant components.

Consistency must be automatically maintained between artifacts within all lifecycle stages. In particular, changes must be constrained by or propagated to, as appropriate, dependent artifacts in other stages.

Activities of the lifecycle, particularly during later stages, should be automated to the extent possible. Techniques include automated code generation of "construction" deliverables and knowledge-based synthesis of design artifacts from analysis.

5.2. Behaviour

A model of objects should rigorously specify behavioral and static semantics. The model should rigorously and declaratively specify concepts of states, events, triggers, operations, attributes, constraints, invariants, pre-conditions, post-conditions, interactions, business rules, and transactional integrity.

5.3. Relationships

Some forms of business semantics can be expressed using the inter-object relationship concepts of a relationship model.

The relationship model within EIM enables specification of complexity-reduction concepts such as **virtual attributes** and **virtual functions** (Bapat, 1994). These concepts simplify usage of the EIM by enabling attributes or functions to "appear" as if they belonged in one object type, but are actually executed in a related object type (possibly via multi-staged relationship traversal). Similarly, **virtual relationships**, based on semantics of role-pairs, can be used to capture indirect relationships within a single specification element. Virtual relationships can be used to clarify or refine business semantics when specializing objects.

Aggregates are complex object types consisting of simpler object types called components. Components may themselves be aggregates. The concept of aggregation is a special case within the General Relationship Model. There is no semantic differentiation between aggregation and other forms of relations. Aggregation should be used within EIM to aid in hierarchically structuring solutions based on one or more perspectives of a problem domain. The EIM should allow specification of several independent aggregation hierarchies. Components may appear in one or more independent aggregation hierarchies. Within each aggregation hierarchy:

- A component can appear in one or more aggregations.
- Both concrete and abstract components can appear in an aggregation.
- A component in an aggregation can itself be an aggregation.
- Recursive aggregation is permitted (e.g., a component in the aggregation can be the aggregation itself).
- An aggregate has an independently specified cardinality for each of its components.

An aggregate may be subclassed. The new subclass may extend the aggregation definition by adding new components or subtyping existing components, providing it does not violate any rules of the aggregation superclass, including any cardinality constraints. Aggregates, as a form of relationship, utilize complexity reduction concepts of virtual attributes, functions, and relationships.

5.4. Specialization

EIM specialization/generalization concepts facilitate extensions to the behavioral model through inheritance mechanisms. Constraints on inheritance are well defined from **specialization theory** (Bapat, 1994) and apply to permissible specializations of operations, attributes, states, pre-conditions, post-conditions, etc. Additionally, specialization theory interprets, defines permissible specializations of, and places restrictions on, relationships inherited by objects. These inheritance implications require a level of syntactic and semantic clarity in the object model which is often missing in conventional methodologies and toolsets.

5.5. Context

The roles and responsibilities of enterprise elements can best be expressed within domain-specific contexts (D'Souza, 1994). Domain-specific contexts reduce exposed complexity and enable visualization of semantically related elements. Contexts can be considered a set of overlapping views, or filters, of the Enterprise Integration Model. A context explicitly restricts exposure of enterprise element details, but the semantic constraints of the underlying model are implicitly maintained. Modal contexts may be used to provide controlled exposure (e.g., visual rendering) of model fragments such as nested aggregations.

5.6. Genericity

Genericity is the staged refinement of entire models (see "
Figure 6: Genericity "Inheriting Industrial Models") [**ESPRIT 93**]. The concept uses stepwise instantiation to go from aggregations of generic components, through increasing specializations of business domains, to enterprise, facility, and work area implementations. Genericity is a controlled process which utilizes principles of specialization, inheritance, relationships, and contexts to leverage reusable industrial models and rapidly provision tailored business solutions.

The concept of genericity should be used to specialize the "language" and semantics appropriate for each business domain. The business language should be defined in terms of higher level generic constructs. Subdomain specialization will in turn be defined in terms of domain constructs.

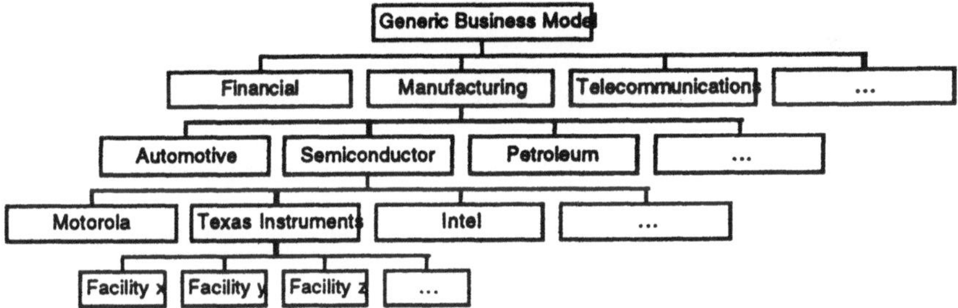

Figure 6:   Genericity "Inheriting Industrial Models"

5.6. Version

All elements within the EIM are continually evolving [**WJ 93**]. Versioning keeps track of the evolution of each EIM element. Closely associated with versioning is configuration management, which manages a set of individual versions of model elements.

5.7. View

View concepts provide the final reduction in exposed surface area and empower the end user to directly interact with the EIM. The view concept is based on **virtual object types** (Bapat, 1994), whose members are completely determined by certain criteria satisfied by members of another object type. The primary mechanisms which form the basis of virtual object types are selection (using arbitrary set-partitioning selection criteria), projection (e.g., list of attributes and functions to be exposed), and conjunction (related object types). Virtual object types are often coupled with security mechanisms to constrain attribute and operational access by end users.

Virtual object types, used in conjunction with other virtualizing concepts can significantly enhance semantic recognition by the end user while reducing or eliminating complexity clutter. The following forms of exposed surface area reduction (complexity hiding) are enabled by these concepts:

- Hiding attributes and operations.
- Hiding relationships by:
    - Compressing multiple object types into single virtual objects.
    - Compressing multiple relationships into single virtual relationships.
- Hiding objects (through selection criteria).

6. Example

As an example of how principles of componentization and the Enterprise Integration Model might work in practice, consider the business needs associated with manufacturing equipment. This single physical component within the enterprise is often viewed from many perspectives, including:

- Manufacturing process. Process specification, material delivery, monitor and control, quality, scheduling, capacity planning, etc.
- Facilities. Spatial requirements, safety, consumable delivery, liquid/gas/power/communication supplies, emergency procedures, installation, etc.
- Financial. Asset inventory, purchase orders, supplier contracts, depreciation, product manufacturing cost, etc.
- Operations. Operator training requirements, skills, scheduling, charge-outs, operating procedures, reprocessing, alignment, handling, etc.
- Maintenance. Parts bill of material, diagnostic procedures, periodic maintenance requirements, equipment performance, etc..

It is not unusual to find these perspectives implemented by completely independent systems which have little or no interoperability. A new business requirement crossing these boundaries may take considerable time to implement and would suffer semantic entropy during the process of communicating business needs to IT provisioners.

In an EIM scenario, each perspective could have been independently evolved, during different time frames, with incremental non-obtrusive implementation strategies. Employing the concepts of specialization and genericity, each perspective may have been independently derived from standard domain models, specialized down to the specific requirements of the work area. Contexts would be used to reduce exposed complexity within each domain while ensuring underlying enterprise model integrity. A new business requirement, which typically involves business rule, workflow, or GUI modification, would have a solution directly implemented by the business user. The business user would implement his solution utilizing EIM-aware tools in conjunction with a combination of EIM views exposing only the relevant business semantics (see "
Figure 7 Example: Using the Enterprise Integration Model").

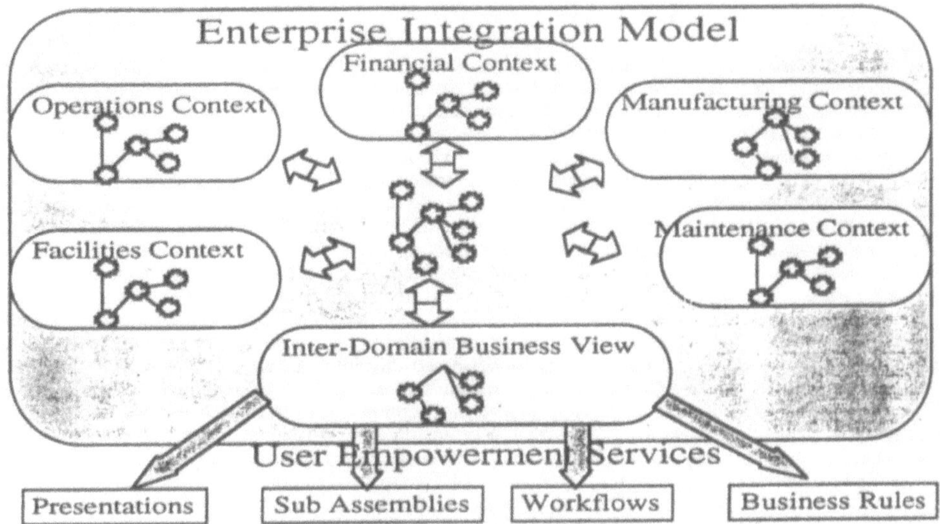

Figure 7 Example: Using the Enterprise Integration Model

7. Semantic Extensions to OMG Standards

OMG's central mission is to establish an architecture and set of specifications to enable distributed integrated applications. Primary goals are the reusability, portability and interoperability of object-based software components in distributed heterogenous environments. Much of the effort to date has been to establish an enabling infrastructure based on open and standard interface definitions. While the enabling infrastructure will have positive impact on the enterprise, orders of magnitude higher impact will be achieved through rapid delivery of interoperable business application components.

Business application components do not exist in isolation. Rigorous and concise semantics are required to ensure enterprise integrity, particularly as empowered users directly provision their business solutions using some form of component assembly paradigm. The Enterprise Integration Model (EIM) embodies a set of tightly coupled concepts necessary to maintain semantic integrity of business application components across the enterprise.

A natural extension of the OMG Architecture would be to formally define business domain facilities in terms of the concepts specified within EIM. Such an architectural extension would:

- Help resolve issues related to semantic integrity of business application components.
- Lay a foundation for an OMG common business infrastructure.
- Create a true plug-and-play business component market.
- Enable implementation of viable end-user solution assembly tools.

An opportunity to incorporate EIM concepts into the OMG Architecture may exist in the form of a BOMSIG initiative. This initiative is soliciting proposals for an OMG standard facility which would serve as the underpinning technology for interoperable business components and many of the concepts referenced in this paper.

8. Conclusion

For many industries, the most compelling business driver for IT is the need for rapid provisioning of business solutions within an environment of increasing complexity. IT organizations are having difficulty meeting these decreasing cycle time requirements, particularly when increased business complexity has an adverse impact on software productivity, quality, cost, and cycle time. The software industry could address these issues by applying concepts of componentization. The benefits of this approach are exemplified by the integrated circuit industry's ability to consistently double producitivity and performance each year. Cycle time reduction goals also require active participation by the business user. Ultimate cycle time reduction will occur when the business user is able to express his problem in a form consistent with his problem domain and have that specification automatically and instantly implemented. Building on component concepts and the need for solution provisioning directly by business users, an open component-based architecture will feature plug and play components and end-user empowerment. This architecture is inherently more complex than contemporary application architectures. The architecture will need to be implemented using a complexity-hiding model-based development approach. Such an approach would iteratively utilize generic constructs forumulated at one level of abstraction as the language and semantic for the next level of specialization. Empowered business users will express their problem in their business language; rapidly provision their solutions; assemble, specialize, and customize business application components. Technology complexity will be hidden, business semantics will be rigorously enforced, and an Enterprise Integration Model will capture the enterprise-specific semantics which allow business application components from multiple business domains to interoperate.

Abbreviations

BOMSIG	Business Object Management Special Interest Group (OMG)
EIM	Enterprise Integration Model
IT	Information Technology
OAG	Open Applications Group
OMG	Object Management Group

References

Subodh Bapat, *Object-Oriented Networks*, Prentice Hall, 1994.

Brad J. Cox, *Object Oriented Programming An Evolutionary Approach*, Addison-Wesley Publishing Company, April 1987.

Brad J. Cox, *Software Technologies of the 1990's*, IEEE Software Magazine, IEEE, November 1990.

Desmond D'Souza, *Object-Oriented Analysis, Modeling, and Conceptual Design*, ICON Computing, Inc, Jan 1994.

ESPRIT Consortium AMICE, *CIMOSA: Open System Architecture for CIM*, Springer-Verlag, 1993.

James Martin, *Rapid Application Development*, Macmillan Publishing Company, 1991.

Object Mangement Group, *Object Analysis and Design*, Draft 7.0, 1 October 1992.

Object Management Group, *The Common Object Request Broker: Architecture and Specification*, Revision 1.2, 29 December 1993.

Object Management Group, Common Facilities Architecture, Revision 4.0, 3 January 1995.

Object Management Group, *Object Services Architecture*, Revision 8.1, 12 January 1995.

Lisa Wirthman, *Time is ticking away*, PC WEEK, July 24, 1995.

Wakeman & Jowett, *PCTE The Standard for Open Repositories*, Prentice Hall, 1993.

Author Index

Ashford, Colin 69

Bennett, Jim E 47

Casanave, Cory 7

Clegg, Dai 77

Digre, Tom 151

Geerts, Guido L 94

Grotehen, Thomas 87

Hertha, William F 47

Kossmann, Rainer 63

McCarthy, William E 94

Page, Ian M 47

Patel, Dilip 1

St Pierre, J A 135

Poirier, Stéphane 69

Post, Frank J 47

Ramackers, Guus 77

Schwaber, Ken 117

Schwarb, René 87

Sims, Oliver 37

Stewart, S L 135

Sutherland, Jeff 1, 29

If you have any concerns about our products,
you can contact us on
ProductSafety@springernature.com

In case Publisher is established outside the EU,
the EU authorized representative is:
Springer Nature Customer Service Center GmbH
Europaplatz 3, 69115 Heidelberg, Germany

Printed by Libri Plureos GmbH
in Hamburg, Germany